Melyssa Hubbard.

Spanking City Hall" retells the unlikely story of a popular big city mayor's effort to take the kink out of the city's leading dominatrix in a classic, Hoosier hysterical moment, only to succeed in rousing a natural revolutionary to rally a diverse group of citizens angered by rising taxes to drive her chief detractor from political office.

The author's blunt and touching candor discussing how she overcame a difficult childhood is inspiring, and she spices things up nicely by sharing with us titillating details about people's unspoken sexual fetishes.

Gary Welsh, attorney & publisher AdvanceIndiana.com

Hubbard's journey from Midwestern dominatrix to the organizer of one of the first Tea Party groups is as fascinating as it is perverse. After the local mayor tried to use her business as a salacious distraction from the city's woes, Hubbard turned her whip on the politician's indecent use of police power, locked him up inside his own vulnerabilities, and, like any good dominatrix, showed him who's in charge when her movement spanked him at the ballot box. You won't be able to put it down."

Bil Browning, award-winning journalist
and publisher of the Bilerico Project

For those familiar with the coverage of Hubbard's war with Indy Mayor Bart Peterson as documented in NUVO (see Paul Pogue's work) and other journals, this is the complete — and completely graphic — backstory. For those unfamiliar with the Circle City's turn of the century morality-play-turned-tax-revolt, it's a cautionary tale for both politicians as they choose their bedfellows and media outlets that decide they're more interested in ginning up outrage than providing substance. There's another fascinating historical subtext, here, as well – the arc of the story as it unfolds over the dawn of the 21st century parallels the explosive growth of the online universe as both a tool and a minefield in the realm of sexual self-expression, discovery and obsession."

NUVO Newsweekly, Indy's Alternative Voice

Hubbard's perversely fascinating account of how she took life and shook it by the lapels is inspiring. It's a handbook of sociopolitical guerrilla tactics, and I couldn't stop reading. Hubbard takes us on a sexually charged journey from vanilla beginnings to a modern tax revolt, ending with a cosmic jolt on the Monument Circle, with clarity and humor. A classic!"

Dave Fulton, Emmy award-winning documentary maker,
Naptown Rock Radio Wars & Videopolis.tv

The Queen of Crops and Wands builds an arresting alternative political universe and narrative that speaks a declarative truth in an era where such is mostly obscured and distorted."

Brian A. Howey, publisher of Howey Politics Indiana

Spanking City Hall

Dominatrix to Political Activist

By Melyssa Hubbard

with John Hausen

Published & distributed by:

Melyssa Hubbard

in association with:

IBJ Book Publishing

41 E. Washington St., Suite 200

Indianapolis, IN 46204

www.ibjbp.com

Library of Congress Control Number: 2013957834

ISBN 978-1-939550-05-7

First Edition

Printed in the United States of America

Disclaimer: This story of my work as a dominatrix, tea party leader, and tax activist is true to the best of my recollection. While this memoir is based on my real experiences, some storylines and events are slightly altered or merged. All names are altered, unless permission is granted to use the person's name, or the person is a public figure.

For Grandma Lola Hubbard who
brought light into my life
and who would never have judged me for the
unusual path to self-actualization I chose.

—Melyssa Hubbard

TableofContents

Preface

I understood I was a little off-kilter and stranger than the average person, but I had been taught the Constitution protected and gave me the right to be different as long as I didn't infringe upon the rights of others. This belief was the master key to a strange journey that rigorously tested that constitutional right and led me to face my worst fears.

One day a friend showed me an online AOL chat room called Dominant Women. I couldn't make sense of my fascination with the subject of dominance and submission (D/s), but I got busy learning as much as I could about it. I wanted to find out why a man would give up control and let a woman dominate and humiliate him. I began to get involved with the D/s subculture online and then got into some real life D/s relationships. Eventually I became a professional dominatrix, built a stellar dungeon in my basement and opened a D/s boutique that sold erotic gear and art, all the while trying to further my education about this weird new world.

Many of my clients were lost, frightened individuals who came to me in the dark of my dungeon for an experience they couldn't fulfill in the light of day. I soon realized that if I could help them face their fears and accept themselves for who they were as individuals, then my own quest to evolve and self-actualize would continue. I saw myself as a legitimate educator of D/s.

Unexpectedly my lifestyle was outed to the media and police and the city inspected my D/s boutique and home. City Hall slapped me with a lawsuit that didn't mention its real motives in trying to shut me down. The underlying reasons involved layers of intolerance and politics as usual. Both my home dungeon business and the inventory in my shop in the Chatham Arch area of Indianapolis had been found legal by inspectors and the police.

I was discreet in my practice and knowledgeably counseled clients about their needs and fears. I was an entrepreneur and professional businesswoman. I didn't cave in but fought the lawsuit and stood up for my rights.

In 2007, Indiana was hit by a political crisis when unfair property taxes were levied. I was ready to fight again and make enough noise that the government would listen. I began by organizing one rally and then meetings and protests which led to starting the first grassroots Tea Party movement in Indianapolis. Right before the mayoral election, we dipped a giant tea bag full of unfair property tax assessments into the Central Canal.

The public outcry got the legislature's attention and property taxes were capped, saving taxpayers more than $1.5 billion as of this writing. Deeply offended by City Hall's agenda against me, I had fought the mayor's re-election and helped his opponent win. Finally, the lawsuit against me was dropped.

This memoir gives the details of my extraordinary, sometimes formidable and always bizarre journey leading to profound spiritual revelations, personal healing and self-actualization.

ChapterOne

A well-built man wearing a Polo shirt and pressed jeans came into my shop to schedule a session with me, Miss Ann, as I was known then. He waited a few minutes to speak to me as he looked at the shop's steel human-sized bird cage, surrounded by racks of leather whips, restraints, collars, cuffs, blindfolds, hoods and the like. The air smelled of leather and rose incense.

I told Don, not his real name, that I charged one hundred dollars for a pre-session interview to determine his experience and needs. Another reason I conducted interviews was to screen out potential creeps and problem clients. If we mutually agreed to schedule a session, the fee was three hundred and fifty dollars. Don handed me a hundred dollar bill and agreed to come back a couple of hours later when I was free to talk with him in depth.

My retail shop, The Reformatory Boutique, was a BDSM (Bondage-Discipline-Sadism-Masochism) emporium located in a quaint, turn-of-the-century neighborhood near downtown Indianapolis. Tucked inside a building that housed artist studios and a contemporary fine art gallery,

THE REFORMATORY
INDIANAPOLIS

I had no storefront so customers had to ring a doorbell to enter. Whether they were into kink or simply curious, customers could come in and explore their fantasies and secret selves in a safe environment. We could have a chat about dominance and submission (D/s) that they wouldn't have in most social situations.

When Don returned, we walked together down East Street to the neighborhood coffee shop to talk and sat at one of the outside tables. I asked him what he was looking to gain from the experience. He was upfront. "Perform oral sex on you," he said. "I also want to have an orgasm." Don with his buzz cut and tattoos wanted to do some oral. He was a man on a mission for sex.

Usually an interviewee would acquiesce and understand the inappropriateness of asking such a thing of a dominatrix. It's not the place of a session submissive to ask for sex . . . ever. In all my years as a professional dominatrix, most would-be clients either hung up the phone or politely excused themselves when they heard my rules on sex. But this man would not relent in his quest.

"I'm a femme domme," I told him, "and that means I ultimately decide what happens in a session, within your limits of course. My limits are penetration, direct sexual contact and anything else outside the letter of the law."

He didn't seem to get it.

"I am a guide, an artist and teacher of D/s." I went on to say upfront that I would keep his money for the interview and my time, but that I did not feel it was wise for him to spend three hundred fifty dollars for a session because he wasn't going to get what he wanted.

He surprised me by saying that he wanted to learn what I taught. I had adopted the maitresse archetype (French for teacher) as my domme role. Other dommes took on personas like nurse, goddess, nun, mother or another dominant female archetype that suited their style. As a maitresse, when someone asked to learn, I felt I could not ethically refuse the session.

Against my better judgment, I agreed to accept Don as a client. However, I warned him that he probably wouldn't like the session. I asked for a deposit for the session and told him to be punctual and not to forget the balance of his fee. As was customary, I also asked if he had any health issues. When Don said he had asthma and used an inhaler, I told him to bring his inhaler or there would be no session. It's the role of the domme to protect the submissive at all times. I gave him my home address and repeated, "Don't be a minute late or a minute early."

Two days later Don rang my doorbell right on time. That was the only thing he got right that day. In my world I knew he was not going to be the norm. I answered the door in my usual black business suit with pencil skirt, long jacket, silk blouse, stockings, garters and high-heeled boots which made me a commanding six-three. I had never felt the need to wear a lot of fetish attire. Sure, I had shiny thigh-high boots, fishnets and corsets but I rarely wore them. Other dommes pulled that look off much better. I preferred instead to look as polished and business-like as possible. I didn't want to wear costumes that would encourage fantasies I had no intention of fulfilling.

I invited Don into the Craftsman-style home I had bought and renovated in an elegant old neighborhood. Two doors down the street stood an Italianate Catholic church.

As soon as I closed my front door, I was in character. "Kneel now, right here on this rug. Do you have the rest of your tribute for me?" I asked. "Put the money in your mouth and clasp your hands behind your back. This is how you properly present tribute to your domme." I took the cash and patted him on the head. "Good boy. Now show me your inhaler."

He thanked me and called me ma'am. He had to be ex-military, I thought, because he seemed trained to use the word ma'am. I instructed him to only address me as

Main photo used to advertise my practice

Miss or Miss Ann. Subs needed to learn that lesson on day one. I always stuck to my rules and quickly took control. Establishing my role as the boss upfront set the tone for a submissive.

I left the room to lock up the money. When I returned, I instructed Don to go into my dining room with its velvety green walls and dimly lit chandelier and sit at the massive walnut table. There I began to discuss protocol for the session since he didn't have the slightest clue about D/s or BDSM, let alone the complex rules for setting the scene, or what's called scening. D/s sessions are essentially living theater so they're called scenes. They're psychological labyrinths where an opposite reality is often true, a world where bondage is freedom and pain is pleasure.

As a total novice, Don needed a verbal education in the art of D/s first. Since he'd been incessantly sex-minded, I was compelled to explain that often sex occurs between individuals who practice D/s as a lifestyle, but within the context of a professional session like ours, my role was to teach protocol and perform physical acts allowable by law and within my client's limits. These physical acts would be a far cry from what he initially requested.

I spent more than an hour giving instruction on everything he needed to know to be prepared, including the proper use of a safeword in the event he experienced either physical or psychological harm outside what he felt he could withstand. It's a word that would end the scene immediately. I made him aware that as a badge of honor there were some experienced submissives who refused to safeword. I also explained he was not one of them.

I shared some of my experiences with boyfriends who were not clients and told him why those relationships were different. I explained that professional dommes, like me, mostly sessioned with novices. Often we're the ones to give submissives an introduction to D/s and BDSM so that they have a safe platform, without strings, to explore.

"Aspects of D/s are in every relationship if you look closely enough," I said.

Don said he understood the rules. Although I remained skeptical, I took his hand and led him to the dungeon in the basement of my home. It was dark with Gothic decor and appropriately outfitted with a bondage table, whipping cross, spanking bench, stockade and eyebolts sunk into the concrete floor, walls and rafters. A large collection of implements such as floggers and whips hung from heavy steel chains. The multi-colored track lights, candle sconces, burgundy velvet pillows, Persian wool rug and steel jail cell made clients feel they had escaped reality. Stepping into my dungeon transported them to a frightening, yet intriguing, dim and other-worldly place.

Although I had just laboriously schooled Don on the rules, my protocol for scening and every aspect of his inaugural session, he didn't even make it down the stairs

Don was a vice cop sent to proposition me for sex and if I complied, arrest me for prostitution.

without propositioning me again for sex. How did he not get it? No means no. This made me furious. In D/s, a relationship is based on consent from all parties and Don's lack of respect for my limits was immoral. I'd worked in jobs before where I was sexually harassed and I wasn't going to tolerate it–especially at my place of business where I had control.

"Stand, don't move. Put your hands behind your back now!" I commanded. "I am in charge and you will do only as I instruct. Do I make myself clear?"

"Yes, Mistress."

"Yes, what?" I shouted.

"Yes, Miss," he said.

To me, the word mistress insinuated adultery. I abhorred this implication because I had remained celibate during my years as a professional domme. As an unmarried woman, the only acceptable title was Miss. My clients all knew this and were informed upfront (as was Don) that this strictly enforced protocol was a pet peeve of mine.

I opened the heavy wooden armoire in the dungeon and removed two trashy lingerie outfits. I showed them to Don and told him he could choose between the two-piece or the one-piece halter-thong. He chose the two-piece. Then I explained that I was going to leave the dungeon for no more than five minutes and when I returned, he was to have neatly put his clothing in the armoire, be dressed in the two-piece lingerie set, and be waiting for me as a prostrate submissive kneeling with his head down on the floor and his rear-end pointed toward the dungeon stairs. I told him the first thing I wanted to see when I came back downstairs was his ass because I now owned it.

When I returned, the first order of business was Don's inspection. A first-time submissive stands before his domme so that she can inspect any crevice or aspect of the sub she wishes to view. Sometimes, subs are naked. Don was crouching as told in his lingerie.

"Stand up, you little creep, and let me take a look at you," I said.

He had quite a few tattoos so I asked what they meant. He explained his tats were symbolic of the universe and creation. I had trouble reconciling how this guy could be capable of deep thinking, let alone have a sense of honor and respect for the universe. The tats were cool. Don was not. His well-placed ink did not change that fact one bit.

I presented my leather training collar, required of all submissives in session, and asked him if he knew what it was.

"It is a collar, Miss."

"Do you know the meaning of the collar and why it's used in training?"

"No, Miss."

In all my sessions I taught that a collar designated symbolic control and ownership and that it was considered an honor for a submissive to wear one. This aging, nearly naked man was clearly getting nervous. His over-sunned, ruddy complexion looked even more pink and his muscles tightened and tensed. By that time a real submissive would have become visibly aroused, even a nervous one, but Don had no erection.

I locked the collar on his neck with a luggage padlock and key, clipped a leash to it and gave it a little yank as I softly assured him that he was mine and his lessons were about to begin. Just like luggage, a sub was something I owned. I guided him to stand in front of a large gold gilt mirror on the far wall. He needed to look at himself in the lingerie. Then I locked sheep's wool-lined leather cuffs for restraint on his wrists and ankles with real padlocks. The keys hung from a sterling chain around my neck.

I pushed his wrists above his head and tied them to eyebolts in the rafters and secured his ankle restraints to bolts in the concrete floor. I owned him physically then. He was strung up with his hands and arms in the air, unable to touch me. I sensed him trembling and grew excited by his fear of me. I had him in my complete control but maintained a cool demeanor. From that point forward, I was consumed with exacting revenge and teaching him a lesson he would likely think about many times.

So there was Don and his tribal tats, wearing tacky lingerie, strung up in a domme's basement, unable to escape and practically unable to move. It was delicious. Next, I walked to the armoire, pulled out a tube of bright red lipstick and showed it to my apprehensive student as I smacked his ass with a black leather crop. I smeared the paint on his mouth so he looked something like a

> "What would your macho buddies think of you now if they could see you helpless and humiliated in my dungeon?"

clown. For a moment I had a flashback of my mother doing the same thing to me as a five-year-old when she believed I had played with her make-up. She humiliated me and threatened to take me in public with lipstick all over my face.

I began my interrogation and asked Don if he liked becoming the slut he wanted me to be. I lit a cigarette and blew the smoke in his face as I paced in circles around him like a cat, toying with her prey.

"What would your macho buddies think of you now if they could see you helpless and humiliated in my dungeon? Does becoming my slut make you feel good about yourself? Is this experience filling you with self-esteem? How do you feel now about treating me like a whore?"

I scrawled the words "slut" and "fuck me" backwards in lipstick on his chest so he could see his humiliation in the mirror. I forced him to stare at himself and asked over and over if he felt good about himself transformed into a slut like he wanted me to be for him.

"No," he mumbled. He looked incredulous as if he didn't understand what was going on.

I thought he might cry. I wanted him to cry. I wanted to hear him sob and see pathetic tears stream down the face of this man who had no respect for women or for me. I dragged the verbal berating on for at least forty-five minutes until my feet started hurting from pacing the concrete floor in my high-heeled boots.

Eventually I let him out of the bondage. I barely gave him aftercare, which means providing warmth and comfort to the sub after a physically intensive session. Subs inspired their level of aftercare. Aftercare always transported me back to my childhood when my mother beat me because she believed I had touched something that was not supposed to be touched or committed some other minor crime. When she realized she had punished me by mistake, she scooped me up and held me in her arms, telling me how sorry she was. I endured those habitual beatings just to be cradled and soothed afterward.

As Don was leaving the dungeon, he again propositioned me for sex! He asked if he became a regular client would I break the rules for him? It was only the fact that we were no longer in a scene that stopped me from striking his face to shame him. After he left, I was happy to finally be rid of him and have his money tucked away in my safe upstairs.

As it turned out, Don was a vice cop sent to proposition me for sex and if I complied, arrest me for prostitution. The operation was part of series of police actions designed to shut down selected small businesses in the city. This confrontation would push me to play out in public a political D/s scene with the city that was far more intense than I could have ever imagined. I would then have no choice but to demonstrate my skill of dominance, honed in my underground dungeon and wielded in the full light of day.

ChapterTwo

I wasn't always a domme who knew how to make an undercover man crawl. I didn't have a clue about D/s eight years earlier. That was in the mid-nineties. I was unaccomplished and didn't own a house. I rented a downtown Indianapolis apartment with beamed ceilings, original oak built-ins and hardwood floors. The place was furnished with modest pieces I'd thrifted over the years at auctions, second-hand stores and yard sales. My moveables were simple and a small art collection hung on the exposed brick walls. In those days I lived hand-to-mouth and party-to-party.

In the winter of 1996, my co-worker Keith lost his apartment when the building was sold so I invited him to move into my spare room for a while. Gay and a blast to be around, I loved going with him on his party circuit. Keith was a reader so his magazines piled up on my coffee table after a couple months. One Saturday morning as I looked through a cooking magazine, Keith's *Utne Reader* caught my eye. On the back cover of the 1996 January-February edition was a short piece written by the now famous

Marianne Williamson. In it she wrote that our power is the one thing that most intimidates us mere mortals. By allowing our flame to burn bright, she wrote, we liberate others from their fear. Her words gave permission for us to be true to who we were as individuals. I knew I had discovered a profound truth.

This piece was published in Williamson's 1992 book *A Return to Love: Reflections on The Principles of a Course in Miracles*. The original book, *A Course in Miracles* by Helen Schucman, guided readers in achieving spiritual transformation. When I read Williamson's words, a sense of calm came over me. I had friends who walked into their fears and revealed to the world their true selves. They took risks and sometimes failed but never shrank from their identities. A conquering lawyer, a budding journalist, a destitute artist–all unique in profession but the same in authenticity.

I was heavy into new age books then and read anything I could find on spirituality and philosophy. A few months earlier, I'd finished reading James Redfield's *The Celestine Prophecy*, and my mind was fresh with the book's first-person spin on eastern traditions and spiritual awakenings. One idea that resonated with me was synchronicity. A major motif in the story revolved around the main character's awareness of life's coincidences and that their significance should never be ignored. I wasn't really doing much with my life back then and I was on high alert for the wind to blow me something with meaning. At the time I couldn't have guessed that I would one day face a formidable journey requiring all the courage and creativity I possessed.

Labor Day, 2000, my artist boyfriend moved out of the 1920's fixer-upper I had just bought, thinking we would live there and renovate it together. I felt abandoned. After a couple of months of feeling sorry for myself and getting over Thacher, I was ready to emerge from my cocoon, at least online. I met and started email correspondence with a guy who called himself Catbird. His real name was Alan. After a few weeks, we decided to meet in person for a beer at the Red Key Tavern not far from my house. This led to more dates and one evening I invited him back to my place. He followed me into my sunroom office, sitting down at my computer before I could check my email.

"Here, let me show you something," he said, pulling up a list of chat rooms. He searched the menu for adult and special interest areas then selected Dominant Women and Submissive Men.

I didn't even know what those terms meant. "What on earth are you doing?" I said, laughing.

"This is really crazy stuff," he said. "These people are all into some kinky shit."

Alan thought it would be funny if he created a screen name and profile for a fake dominatrix and entered the chat room. It sounded like a hilarious plan to me. We entered the Dominant Women chat room and scrolled down the monitor to see users bantering back and forth about flogging, bondage, gags, and from what I could tell, some other pretty racy activities. Alan explained D/s had unique capitalization. The capital "D" signified the higher position of the dominant and small "s" denoted the lower station of a submissive.

IndySpankDom was the alias he created for our dominatrix. To draw attention he dangled his mistress screen name in the buzzing chat room. Obviously, Alan had spent some time there before. He understood how things went down with the accuracy and intensity of a savvy participant. Boys flocked to users identifying themselves as dommes, professing their devotion and begging to submit. Alan said this was standard internet D/s protocol. I found the whole thing fascinating and felt attracted to the weirdness.

After Alan introduced the screen name IndySpankDom to the group, we received about ten brrrings in the first couple minutes. Our screen was full of instant messages from guys dying to chat with IndySpankDom. The first conversation he dove into was with BearsFan. Alan beamed as he took command. I saved the first instant message D/s chat held on my computer.

BearsFan: hello Ma'am, looking for Indy boys to spank?

IndySpankDom: Maybe

BearsFan: may I ask where in Indy you are Ma'am?

IndySpankDom: in your basement . . . come down and see me

Alan cracked a smile as I looked over his shoulder. I couldn't believe this was happening. The conversation was bizarre and yet somehow gripping.

> **IndySpankDom:** So john what are you offering?
>
> **BearsFan:** whatever you wish for me to do for you, Ma'am
>
> **IndySpankDom:** don't say whatever . . . you don't know how mean I am john. you might end up in a position you find uncomfortable
>
> **BearsFan:** I will do anything you wish Ma'am
>
> **IndySpankDom:** good . . . you're not the sharpest knife in the drawer are you john?
>
> **BearsFan:** no Ma'am

Alan was great in character and had this guy eating out of his hand. He was taking BearsFan for a ride and knew exactly how to press his buttons.

> **BearsFan:** may I ask what part of Indy are you from, Ma'am?
>
> **IndySpankDom:** be patient john . . . I like you so far. Don't fuck that up. do you have a pic of yourself for me, hopefully one in a compromising position?
>
> **BearsFan:** well I have a pic, but not one in a compromising position Ma'am
>
> **IndySpankDom:** how can I offer you something if you don't have anything to offer me?
>
> **BearsFan:** are you sending me your pic Ma'am?

IndySpankDom: only if you're serious. If you are, write me a letter telling me of a fantasy you have, no shorter than one page. It will be in my inbox when I wake up . . . after that we can talk about our similar interests

BearsFan: If you were serious you'd send your pic, bye

IndySpankDom: you little shit . . . if you were truly a sub you would do me this little favor . . . don't think you will get exactly what you want right away . . . that's not how it works john

His change in tone startled me. Alan had morphed from the sweet guy I'd met for drinks a couple weeks earlier into a hardcore internet dictator. And he did it all as a woman, taking control of a random stranger with a few keystrokes. I was surprised how much Alan's prowess as a dominatrix turned me on. Right then and there, he got under my skin and became the catalyst that launched me into the world of D/s.

After the chat was over, we burst into laughter. The look of delight on his face burrowed into my mind. And that smile. He hadn't let on that he was such a pro on the subject but I craved more. The idea of having permission to be in control was a huge turn on. Before that, I'd had no idea that a man would consent to pure, unadulterated obedience. I knew in that moment I would not stop until I got to the bottom of what made a submissive man tick.

Turns out, Alan wasn't just into D/s when he was

screwing with people online. He desired to be used and confessed he wanted a domme. Specifically, he wanted an intimate relationship with me giving the orders. In all my previous relationships, I pretended to be submissive while in reality, I was trying to control everything. Becoming the domme Alan wanted got me fantasizing.

Since he wanted me to look the part even though I didn't know what I was doing, we began shopping together for my sexy wardrobe. Online he showed me the boots, stockings and garters that got him going. One night he took me out and bought a pale blue satin embroidered bustier for me which I still wear to this day. Before long I found a website specializing in European heeled hosiery. That was more my style, the classics. Alan and I spent an entire evening online, exchanging links back and forth, discussing which items I should have. Large orders were placed. I bought a pair of shiny thigh-high boots, a leather riding crop, handcuffs, garter belts and a dozen pairs of stockings.

When I was lost and did not know how to fully take control, he topped from the bottom, or passed me suggestions. I laughed, thinking of an outsider looking in on Alan and me role-playing. Normally I was sure exactly how to advance, but when I stalled with Alan, he was able to pick things up.

"Why don't you tell me to get on my knees in front of you, Miss," Alan said.

"The idea of having permission to be in control was a huge turn on. Before that, I'd had no idea that a man would consent to pure, unadulterated obedience.

Even though he was really telling me what to do, he wasn't being truly submissive to me unless I was the one in command. I struggled to get into character. When I told him exactly where to put his hands and he willingly complied, the sex was irresistible. I'd never been so intimate with anyone before, not even my former artist boyfriend. From then on Alan and I skipped the small talk and were in bed together quickly every time we saw each other. He was a drug I couldn't stop taking.

Alan wasn't good for me, though, because behind closed doors he had a dark side. We were both emotional wrecks with intense baggage. We went on for six months but he didn't treat me well outside the bedroom. When the sex ended and we got out of character, Alan was absent.

He would head home. He worked hard to please in the bedroom but was incapable of supplementing any of my emotional needs.

Meeting guys on the internet was artificial. I soon learned people could feign who they were for show. Alan was no different. In actuality, his story was quite sad. One spring afternoon he dropped by and finally spilled his truth to me. I'm not sure why he picked that day. A year before we met, he had suffered the unexpected death of his true love and unborn child. Alan's trauma left him unable to develop a deep connection with anyone. I think he liked playing the submissive role in bed because it allowed him to connect intimately with women and not think.

I was compassionate towards Alan's past but his disrespect for me made it so damn hard to stomach his presence. He came over once and picked me up in a vintage Porsche he'd just purchased. A few hours later we were back in front of my house in a heated argument culminating in me slapping his face as hard as I could. I needed love and admiration outside of the bedroom. I loved becoming the domme he wanted, yet the more I attempted to embrace the role, the more distant Alan became. I didn't understand. I missed being in real day-to-day love.

I wanted to get to the bottom of what made subs tick and why they got so much pleasure from serving at a woman's feet. I also wanted to find out what experiences in their pasts might have triggered their fetishes. I was morphing into an anthropologist, studying a group of humans in a bizarre subculture. That was how I saw myself in the beginning.

My first experiments were gauche and awkward, but the internet was anonymous and there was no danger of consequences. Or so I thought at the time when I took control of the new AOL screen name. I was just trying to learn the D/s psychology.

> **SubMike3:** Hi Ma'am! Nice Profile! I am a switch from western Iowa and currently seeking a very strict/harsh domme.
>
> **IndySpankDom:** I am not available to talk with you now, however to show me that you are serious about speaking with a harsh domme, you will send me an email no less than 1 page in length detailing your interests and experiences . . . I will talk with you more later.
>
> **SubMike3:** Yes Ma'am.
>
> **IndySpankDom:** I can see that you are potentially a serious sub . . . I will look for your email no later than tomorrow morning when I have my coffee
>
> **SubMike3:** Yes Ma'am.
>
> **IndySpankDom:** good boy . . . now get to work

I was giddy, chatting as a domme. During breaks, I brushed up on the finer points of D/s so I could hold my own. For instance, I needed to know that a switch was a dominant who had decided to become a submissive, or vice versa. I found a profusion of good information at sexuality.org and literotica.com.

Sexuality.org was a serious sex-education website that helped me understand in-depth the physical aspects of BDSM and the vocabulary. It also published articles about safe play and how a healthy power exchange was supposed to work. Literotica.com published stories mostly authored by anonymous subs with vivid imaginations. They wrote about being stripped of all control by beautiful, powerful women who emasculated them. Their perspective gave me a glimpse into a sub's fantasies. I loved spinning fantasy into reality and learned that a dominatrix could go deeply into strange places during a scene and subs would love it.

Not all the chats were enlightening or interesting. Some were downright frightening. An east coast cop brrring-ed me on AOL instant messenger and told me a really twisted story. JCOR88 had been seriously injured in a D/s scene by a third party, a female domme. His mistress had allowed a female dominant to participate and use him as a toy. This female dominant had ignored his safeword. Rather than arrest the offending domme for assault, his mistress allowed him to do anything he wanted to the domme. It was essentially blackmail.

JCOR88: Mistress, I had her perform public acts meant to humiliate her. Episodes of public nudity, pointing out men in bars ordering her to consent to oral sex in the back room with them.

JCOR88: I did not want to harm her, but to punish her, Mistress

IndySpankDom: and she did the things you asked of her?

JCOR88: She had no choice, Mistress. She would have done that, rather than to be forced to submit in jail. This woman would have certainly been beaten and used as a toy in jail.

IndySpankDom: yes, but didn't she realize that you had no power to proceed with legal action because of your position? would she have been used by the jailors or the other inmates?

JCOR88: I think that she thought I would have fabricated something Mistress. I believe that both would have used her.

IndySpankDom: interesting . . . did you enjoy dominating her or being dominated by her?

JCOR88: The one time being dominated was enjoyable, until the injury. However, I did enjoy dominating her after she had to serve me until I was able to move my arm again.

It was all too bizarre to be made up and something about this submissive's words sounded too serious and matter-of-fact to be anything but the truth. Even after a debilitating injury, he was begging to submit to a domme online. I was shocked these guys opened up to a complete stranger like me.

JCOR88: She wore nothing unless she was to go outside the apartment.

IndySpankDom: what did she do in the apartment to serve you?

JCOR88: She performed every service of housekeeping, as well as pleasing me and whomever I so dictated for her to please. Mistress, I allowed her very little pleasure. It was my contention that she was to be punished. I had her prepare/serve drinks and food to myself and my company. Have I displeased or otherwise offended you Mistress?

IndySpankDom: no you haven't . . . so tell me about the guests at your house . . . were they aware of your lifestyle?

JCOR88: No Mistress, my guests were other police officers. I had them think that I hired an erotic waitress for football games.

IndySpankDom: very nice . . . and they liked that . . . i'm sure. did you force her to be your furniture?

JCOR88: I did Mistress. I was pretty angry Mistress.

When I wasn't socializing with friends or at my job, I was in D/s chat rooms for about six hours a night, trying to get subs to reveal how they thought about themselves, their fantasies and fears. The chats escalated as I got more comfortable with my role as domme/pseudo-therapist. One day I met a married lawyer named Arthur. We chatted over the next several months. He brazenly discussed cheating on his wife whom he often referred to as plain. In one chat he called his girlfriend-on-the-side a dumb vanilla fuck. His contempt for women was reprehensible. He seemed to be in it purely for himself with no sense of morality. I never considered meeting MRATTY in real life but as with every one of my subjects online, I wanted to see how far I could go with him. I wanted to hear his stories because his attitudes and lack of conscience seemed sociopathic. He was a fascinating study. As always, I made sure to keep a safe distance from lunatics.

MRATTY: can I ask you one thing please?

IndySpankDom: always address me as Ma'am.

MRATTY: Sorry Ma'am. can I ask yu one thing Ma'am?

IndySpankDom: "yu" or "you"?

MRATTY: Can I ask you one thing, Ma'am? Sorry Ma'am. I tried to correct it Ma'am

IndySpankDom: that is better, Arthur.

MRATTY: I want oto be fucked and abused like a little slut, Ma'am

IndySpankDom: it that "oto" or "to," Arthur? I keep record of your mistakes very carefully, do you understand?

MRATTY: I understand Ma'am. What do you do with that record, Ma'am?

IndySpankDom: Do you practice law so sloppily, Arthur?

MRATTY: No Ma'am. It is just that you have me so excited Ma'am

IndySpankDom: I teach grammar to bad boys

MRATTY: I have made a huge wet spot in the front of my pants from leaking Ma'am and my hands are shaking from the excitement, Ma'am. I am very sorry, Ma'am

IndySpankDom: I want you to write a profile before we talk again. I am signing off now

MRATTY: What must be in it Ma'am. I am sorry Ma'am

IndySpankDom: that is up to you, but make it interesting. you can email tomorrow with your experience.

Arthur personally repulsed me, but I wanted to peer inside the mind of a man who cheated and treated women, even me, with disdain and disrespect.

MRATTY: I need to serve someone who knows hoe to do it, Ma'am

IndySpankDom: I know you do, Arthur, but you haven't proven yourself to me yet. You can't even get a simple line of text right. Is that "hoe" or "how"? Do you see what I mean? You're a fucking failure. You are an attorney, for God's sake!

MRATTY: My hands shake when I talk to you Ma'am. I am sorry, Ma'am

IndySpankDom: look I don't care if your hands shake . . . proofread! think about how I feel when you click the send button and there is a misspelled word. It makes me think you really don't care about how well you serve me. Do you ever see misspelled words or typos in my text? Do I have to refresh your memory, or are you really that stupid?

MRATTY: Not stupid, Ma'am. My hands get shakey, but only when dealing with you, Ma'am

IndySpankDom: What would happen in real life then? You would be careless in how you serve me. If i asked you to paint my toenails, you would get polish on my feet or my bed.

MRATTY: No Ma'am

IndySpankDom: If I instructed you to clean my bathroom, you would miss the corners . . . it's all tied in together . . .

Arthur later revealed to me he bought a sex toy for his girlfriend. He said he never would have spoken of such a thing to his wife. His girlfriend didn't catch on at first that the personal pleasure object was actually for him.

MRATTY: Hello Ma'am. My panties are tight as hell

IndySpankDom: I can't talk now, Arthur I'm signing off. I'm glad those panties are tight, I hope they are choking your scrotum . . . you are filthy

MRATTY: Why can't you talk now Ma'am? You can never talk to me, Ma'am Could I phone you Ma'am?

IndySpankDom: I am going to a concert tonight . . . no you can't phone me, I'm very busy

MRATTY: What concert Ma'am? Do you have any intention of meeting for a real time session? I am not really into cyber training, Ma'am

IndySpankDom: you haven't proven yourself to me yet, Arthur.

MRATTY: My girlfriend is not into the scene at all Ma'am

IndySpankDom: did you ask her to?

MRATTY: Yes, Ma'am. She freaked out Ma'am

IndySpankDom: she did, huh? Did you show the toy to her?

MRATTY: Yes Ma'am. I really wantd to give it to you, though, Ma'am

Arthur could not be helped. I was repulsed by his selfish obsession with his little brain and his deranged relationships with women, but Arthur opened my eyes to the extreme secret lives some men led. I said a prayer for his wife and exited his cyber life forever.

I never had any intention of meeting these online subs. Not an inkling of interest. They offered but it was just too freaky and I refused to even send any of them my photo. As one of the few femme dommes in the group, I was constantly hit with chats from a litter of boys looking for attention. TiedUpToday didn't talk to me about anything extraordinary right away. He said he was local but I didn't care. I was domming these guys online to get into the psyche of a submissive man, trying to explore what was out there, not to experience D/s in the flesh. Not yet, anyway. TiedUpToday was bland and I had kinkier guys online to study. I closed his chat box.

Then TiedUpToday surprised me with an unexpected

fetish he wanted to share. He was into being tied up and was a connoisseur on the subject of jeopardy bondage. This kind of bondage meant rigging a knot so that when the sub squirmed, the knot tensed. I would use a form of jeopardy bondage on the undercover cop five years later.

The more we talked, the more he sounded like a guy I had once dated who hung around the downtown art scene and was easily recognizable by a particular cocktail. I asked what his favorite drink was.

"Pernod," he wrote.

It WAS Liam! He invited me to meet him at midnight on the steps of the church by my house. That night under the intense moonlight, he looked cuter than I remembered.

"I knew it was you!" I said.

"I knew it was you, too. Long before you figured it out."

We walked over to my front porch to have a glass of wine and catch up. When we had first dated, our chemistry fizzled and we went our separate ways. Meeting again, we had something new in common and were eager to hear stories about the other's D/s experiences. Talking with Liam about exploring the lifestyle excited me. I needed someone different than the online subs to take me further inside D/s. Liam was safe. He was someone I knew, respected and could trust.

I didn't let on how good looking I thought Liam was. He was charmingly insecure about his looks and exuded a vulnerability that humanized him, a great underlying attribute for a sub. Liam's hip style wore well on his athletic frame. His hair, soft and loose, hung in his face a tinge. Liam and I got together in the following months to explore our inner D/s selves and play with ropes. He helped me understand the sensual side of D/s and bondage. Scening with Liam wasn't scary. Because I trusted him, I allowed him to blindfold me early on. I learned first-hand that when sight and movement were restricted, pain and pleasure intensified. I was drunk off every sensation. It was a mind-blowing revelation.

Like Alan, Liam was a submissive who topped from the bottom to teach me how to lead. Over time I didn't need instruction. I grew comfortable taking control of him.

"For someone who is brand new at this, you are incredibly fearless," Liam told me. "No one has ever taken me down so effortlessly." He said I was a natural and suggested I do it professionally. "Guys would pay good money to scene with you."

Domming for fun on the weekends was one thing, but earning a living doing D/s seemed completely out of the question.

Liam's suggestion startled me. He had to be joking! The idea made my stomach churn, particularly the attached social stigma. I did not want to be labeled a whore or a prostitute and be judged. Liam told me his biggest fear was being outed for his kink. He was completely paranoid himself. Sounded like a whole lot of trouble. Domming for fun on the weekends was one thing, but earning a living doing D/s seemed completely out of the question.

I didn't know what the future held but D/s was becoming more of an obsession each day. When I was alone, I explored more deeply my new role as a domme. While I did not want to become a professional domme, Liam's suggestion did make me curious. What would it be like to scene with other guys? He proposed I go out and get as much experience as I could. I figured Alan and Liam were both single, good looking and brainy. There had to be more out there like them.

I was no longer just an internaut domme, I was turning into the real deal and it was exciting. I told some of my friends about it and they thought I was nuts. I didn't care. These relationships fed my intellect and power exchange games were intoxicating. I was going in deeper.

Chapter Three

My early childhood was as normal as any kid's who lived with a single mom in a poor neighborhood. I grew up with my younger sister, Cindy, in the early sixties in a small Indiana factory town named Palmerton. Entire families transplanted themselves to our town from poor southern states for jobs in one of the four main manufacturing plants. My hometown was a working-class Peyton Place, rife with bed-hopping, extra-marital affairs, divorces, drugs and alcohol.

My mother spent some of the thirty years she worked for the factory hunched over a microscope. The factory employed 30,000 people, about half the town. Circuit boards for car radios were manufactured there and she worked an assembly line, soldering tiny wires, using a microscope. Bond, repeat. Bond, repeat. She hated the job and the inefficiency of the union-controlled company, but the wage and benefits were good. Some days, entire shifts were wasted on bad parts with Mom performing the next step on circuit boards already known to be defective.

Mom met my biological father while teaching dance

lessons at the local Arthur Murray studio. He was supposedly well-educated and successful by Palmerton standards, but she didn't tell him when she got pregnant. She said their relationship wasn't serious so she didn't want to burden him. He never knew about me. I was supposed to be given up for adoption but after Mom held me, she said I was so pretty she couldn't bear to give me away. My first year, I lived mostly with my grandma because my mother needed help caring for me.

Grandma was the most important person in my life. We formed a strong bond and I believe we shared many lifetimes together. Because I was born on George Washington's birthday, February 22, Grandma marked me early in life as a patriot by making me custodian of the family flag in 1968 when I was six. I was always made to feel special when I was young because of my Washington connection. Grandma died a physical death in 2003, but is with me every single day. I keep shrines with pictures of her around my house and still hear her voice. I have a small vintage painting of Jesus, hanging in my room for her.

She showed me by example how to live life with honor and kindness. In the early seventies, Grandma helped jump-start the Interracial Friendship Group of black and white ladies. Following her lead I had a circle of girlfriends in grade school who were black. They were smitten with my long blond hair and loved to brush it. I was tall and skinny, outgrowing my teachers by sixth grade which made kids poke fun at my height, calling me names like giraffe and bean pole. My girlfriends always had my back when someone picked on me.

Every morning I walked a mile to grade school, passing the small untidy homes lining my street. I always sensed I didn't belong on the wrong side of the tracks and acted like I was destined for bigger things. Exactly what, I didn't know, but it certainly would be grander than living among the people in my neighborhood. The other kids didn't appreciate my uppity attitude and I was targeted by bullies.

When I was in high school and friends from better parts of town visited me, I was embarrassed by my neighborhood. I loved sleepovers at my girlfriends' homes because their houses were nicer than mine. The places where I babysat as a teenager often smelled putrid. I was a popular babysitter because I spent entire evenings tidying up and washing mountains of nasty, crusty dishes and pots and pans left on countertops for days. The caked-on grease and grime were impossible to scrub off the stovetops.

The house we lived in until I graduated high school was a white aluminum two-story. Being unmarried with four children, mom needed Grandpa to co-sign the mortgage. The house cost ten thousand dollars and the monthly payment was one hundred ten dollars. We moved there after my twin half-brothers came to live with us when I was four. The two bedrooms upstairs had no hallway so my brothers walked through the room I shared with my sister Cindy to get to theirs. Since there was no heat in our rooms, we could see our breath in winter and a layer of frost covered the inside of the windows. We survived nights with heavy blankets. In summer the upstairs got so hot, we took bedding downstairs and slept on the floor in front of the only fan we owned.

> "A lot of people in town must have known we had different dads. Women who had children by different fathers were thought of as whores or, at best, unsavory women.

My family of five shared a tiny bathroom in the back of the house that I can only describe as janky. It worked most of the time and was kept clean, but the floor was rotting out and the toilet rocked when anyone sat on it. The only place to bathe was a small metal stand-up shower. Sometimes big fat, ugly garden slugs crawled up through the shower drain.

Grandma's house on the corner was always immaculate. I was lucky to have her close by as I grew up. Years earlier she and grandpa had remodeled and installed plush carpeting and wallpaper. The house was airy and her modern bathroom was stocked with elegant lotions, soaps, lip balms and perfumes. A pot of homemade soup was almost always in the kitchen. She kept large tins full of homemade cookies, fudge, peanut brittle and brownies dusted with powdered sugar on the cold porch. In summer when I spent the night at her house, Grandma outfitted the cold porch with a daybed and crisp, fragrant linens.

The front porch was furnished with a wooden swing and plenty of seating for anyone who might drop by. Surrounded by an array of beautiful flowers, friends and family would visit for hours, reminiscing over tea or lemonade. At five years old I shocked everyone by looking up at Grandma and saying, "Poor old Grandma doesn't have loooong for this world."

Grandma was in her fifties but seemed ancient to me. I was afraid of losing her and not prepared to live in a world without her. She ran the nursery always full of kids at the church right across the street. I loved Sundays because I volunteered to help babysit toddlers and infants while their parents attended church. During the services we made play-dough cookies and sang bible songs. At an early age I learned how to properly change a diaper.

Grandma's first husband was Mom's father. He was abusive and once threatened to kill both my mom and her. Somehow Grandma got a judge to exile him from Palmerton. I was told that's how things were done in small towns back then. Grandma was adamant that she would never let a man disrespect her and always held her ground as an independent woman. She was the matriarch. She got remarried to a wonderful man who treated my mother as one of his own.

Mom never really knew her biological father but heard he had relocated to Florida, so when she was nineteen, she left Palmerton to find him. In Florida mom got pregnant with twins and married their father but the marriage only lasted a short time. It was never clear why she lost custody of the boys and returned to Indiana.

Childhood for Cindy and me was okay until our older half-brothers came to live with us. They had been living with their paternal grandfather in the wilds of central Florida, roaming the marshes like feral children. Apparently they had no supervision. One day mom left us in Grandma's care and a few days later, she returned with a U-Haul and two ten-year-old boys who were wild. Everything was about to change.

Years later, Mom took Cindy and me to a gala at a Victorian mansion the local historical society had renovated. I was in fifth grade. The mansion had been transformed into a museum, capturing the city's opulent industrial-era boom, and was listed on the National Register of Historic Places. After touring the mansion, we went to a neighboring home for the reception. This house had gorgeous peonies in bloom, flowering trees and elaborate decor with fine antiques, all foreign to the

Palmerton I knew. Cindy and I were dressed in our best clothes because mom wanted to make sure we looked like we belonged with the historical society crowd. I felt like somebody that afternoon.

Then we bumped into a well-dressed woman wearing white gloves. She said, "Your daughters are both such pretty blond, blue-eyed girls."

I noticed Mom looking uncomfortable. Apparently she hadn't seen this woman since around the time I was born.

"It's interesting how they both look like you but odd that they look nothing like each other," the woman went on.

Not understanding the remark, I didn't know why Mom made us leave the party so quickly. On the way home she talked about how she didn't like the woman. She had seemed nice enough to me, but then I had no clue the woman was being malicious, hinting at one of Mom's secrets. A lot of people in town must have known Cindy and I had different dads, but no one talked about it in front of us. In those days, out-of-wedlock births were scandalous. Women who had children by different fathers were thought of as whores or, at best, unsavory women. Mom lived with that stigma. I hadn't yet learned how cruelly people judged one another.

About a week later, Mom called Cindy and me downstairs. We sat quietly on the stairs while she explained that the man whose name was on our birth certificates was not really our dad and that the two of us had different fathers. Mom said their identities didn't matter. What was important was that we knew her, our brothers, our grandmother, aunt and uncle–everyone already in our lives.

With four mouths to feed, Mom depended on work at the factory. She wasn't getting child support and was like the woman who lived in a shoe with too many children. Our unruly brothers pushed her over the edge and she started having psychotic episodes and extremely violent outbursts. I began to live every day in fear. Terror and intimidation took over for normal communication. Mom was unmarried, had four kids, a factory job and her dreams weren't going to come true. The smallest thing set her off.

> " I was ten when I was molested for the first time. Many nights shortly after Mom left for work, the sex games began.

Stressed to the brink, she tore open every drawer in the house, angrily heaving the contents all over the room. She overturned all the furniture and destroyed things. Then she made us stay up for hours, cleaning up the mess. I cried to the point my eyes nearly swelled shut and went to school red-eyed, yet no one guessed that I had been up all night, terrorized by my deranged mother.

Mom beat us with whatever she could get her hands on. Once I was accused of doing something and when I tried to stand up for myself, Mom grabbed a board and bashed me over the head. I felt blood running down my face. She dragged me by my hair to the kitchen sink to wash it off. I can still feel the scar on my scalp. My brothers were so disobedient and disrespectful that their punishments were even worse than mine.

One Saturday mom took me to the local dime store on the town square. She parked in front of the courthouse and told me to wait in the car. It seemed she was browsing the aisles forever so I got out of the car, sat on the hood and lollygagged on the sidewalk. When Mom returned, she was furious.

"I thought I told you to wait in the car!" she yelled. "You're going to get it when we get home!"

At home she went after me with a rawhide bullwhip she'd bought that year at the Indiana State Fair. She put welts on my skinny legs and I ran out of the house screaming. I pounded on the neighbors' doors, crying and begging for help, but no one would call the police.

While Mom worked the second shift, she left my brothers in charge of Cindy and me. They were sixteen and one of them in particular saw me as sexual prey. I was ten when I was molested for the first time. Many nights shortly after Mom left for work, the sex games began. I was stripped, forced to lie down and a blanket was put over my head then I was sexually tortured. Under a burgundy blanket with satin trim, I concentrated on blacking out what was happening between my legs.

"If I only had a father then Mom would not have to go to work and someone would be home to protect me from this," I screamed over and over in my head. "If I only had a father, if I only had a father. If I only had a dad."

I cried for myself every time I was tortured. Mike told me I'd better keep quiet or he would beat me and I knew if I snitched, all hell would break loose. I felt guilty and ashamed enough already, so I said nothing for years. I spent a lot of time crying and a lot of time alone, living in my fantasies. I was a huge Elton John fan and I imagined that he would come to Palmerton and rescue me. It was a weird, irrational fantasy but it made me feel better. I still hate wool blankets with satin edging.

As I grew older, I was mean and picked on Cindy a lot. I harassed her, aping the violence our brothers unleashed on me, and incessantly made fun of how overweight she was. I felt I was better than Cindy every time I berated or hit her. Like me, she suffered in that house and I'm not sure why I added to her hell almost every day. I guess I needed someone smaller to abuse. If I could change anything at all about my life, it would be how I treated Cindy. She has forgiven me, but I am still deeply ashamed and full of regret about what I did.

Then one day my mother's past came back again to haunt us. I had met a nice guy named Troy at the Senior Fling. We hung out together all night at the party inside the locked gymnasium. He gave me a sweet goodnight kiss and asked to take me on a date.

The next morning I told Mom about Troy.

"Troy is your sister's half-brother and they are white trash!" Mom shouted.

I started to cry.

"You are not going out with that boy!"

That was how I learned who Cindy's father was. Even though Mom had illegitimate children and we lived in a poor neighborhood, she considered Troy's family white trash. Troy was nice but our budding romance ended right then and there. I suspected he might have had a bad boy streak in him, a trait that would always attract me.

I put my childhood memories in a strong-lidded box and forgot about them until I was in my twenties. Even then, I didn't deal with the painful abuse and was blind to it being the driving force behind my anger, fear, promiscuity and need for attention.

ChapterFour

Something had happened in 1997 that foreshadowed my future journey into D/s. One night I ran into an old friend I called Uncle Barry. He said he had an unusual request. He wanted me to make a human-sized lady out of salmon mousse. I burst out laughing. I taught cooking and even catered a dinner party for Uncle Barry and his wife once. Within a few months after their party, I created a catering menu and eventually built up a network of clients. I made good money, catering on the side. Uncle Barry's quirky, out-of-nowhere idea sounded fun.

"Of course, I'll make a salmon woman for you," I said.

He told me the mousse sculpture was for an annual visual arts exhibit called the Erotic Arts Show at Fountain Square Theatre. The event founder wanted a sexy appetizer and the producer asked that the hors d'oeuvres mirror an art theme. I accepted, having zero clue how to make a giant sculpture out of fish.

"Someone needs to pay for the salmon," I said.

Uncle Barry snapped off a hundred dollar bill and told me to make it happen.

"Get me a mold, too," I added.

"We'll drop one off this week."

The mold was a hollow, plastic mannequin torso with no arms or legs used for retail wall display. It was going to make the perfect mold. I searched online for a recipe and multiplied the ingredients to make enough to fill the cavity. It took four commercial-sized pans to poach the salmon which I had to do in the cooking school's two ovens. I baked the whole fish filets in a bath of Sauvignon Blanc, lemons and dill. Then back in my apartment I mixed the salmon, cream and other ingredients in every mixing bowl I owned and even borrowed some from my neighbor, Alice.

"The butter is the most important part," I told Alice. "If we don't get enough lubricant on this girl, she's not coming out of the mold in one piece."

If a boob didn't come out right, it was irreparable. Alice buttered the mold for an hour. From that night on, I affectionately called her butter bitch. Another friend Diana helped me load the sculpture into my Nissan to transport it to the show. The mousse not only emerged perfectly from the mold onto a silver platter but it tasted sublime. With her olive nipples and necklace made from grape halves, my salmon lady was an appropriate centerpiece for the 1997 Erotic Arts Show.

The line of people entering the theater door that night never ended. More than a hundred erotic works of art were exhibited by local artists and the kinkier the exhibit, the stranger and more perverse it seemed to me. One of the exhibit rooms had temporary walls inside with peep holes cut out. I watched a male exhibitionist pose in what seemed to me unflattering positions. I felt disgusted yet fascinated at the same time, however, nothing except my own curiosity had made me look inside the live freak show. Kinky was something I didn't understand and a glance into that world was unsettling.

My boyfriend Thacher went with me to the party. He didn't like crowds or parties as much as I did but he had on display a bronze mermaid priced at three hundred dollars and wanted to play the artist role. Thacher went home early and left me behind. I didn't care. I was going to stay out all night and party with the freaks–even if they were sexually uninhibited. That was my introduction to kink in 1997.

Three years later, post-Alan and having soloed in D/s chat rooms, I understood the need to set the right bait to attract subs with different psychologies, fetishes and boundaries. My new screen names, DominaMaitresse and DominatrixMagic, made my profiles easy to find and hard to resist. I was inundated with emails and IM requests.

My quest was to get more experience by scening live with some choice submissives. Primo subs were often found near the coasts so I didn't limit myself to Indianapolis. Part of the thrill was convincing them to visit me on my home turf where I could dictate the environment for lifestyle scening. A few months later, I had sorted out the guys who really wanted to serve and narrowed the list down to four. Each one met my basic requirements, passed my credentials check and seemed sane and safe.

Jeff was a commodities trader who wanted to take me out in Chicago. After weeks of cyber flirting and phone calls, I was itching for a trip to the Windy City. I drove up on a Saturday morning and two-and-half hours later was downtown at his high-rise condo building. We had agreed to meet in the lobby and then walk to a coffee shop. If things weren't cool, I prearranged a potential check-in with a friend and had tentative secondary plans to go see a particular band.

I knew who my man was the minute I walked through the door. Jeff's dark hair and green eyes were sexy. We sizzled over coffee and couldn't stop smiling. Scening looked promising. Things were going smoothly in large part because of all the contact we'd had online and by phone.

Urban and masculine, his place had an uncluttered feng shui feel. It was beautifully renovated and demonstrated his work ethic and competence in multiple disciplines. I loved a renaissance man. As evening approached, Jeff suggested he shake a couple martinis to sip while we continued our talk. Then he brought out two large leather duffel bags bulging with props and toys.

"Look what I do in my spare time!" he said.

Jeff laughed as he showed me his secret treasure. One at a time he proceeded to tell me about every toy in his satchels. I didn't mind. I'd never had such a selection at my disposal. He looked as excited as a kid sharing his baseball card collection. With the toys at our feet, we had a dinner of pizza and a salad. We weren't there for the food.

Afterward I showered and dressed in a black leather dress and floor-length black satin blazer. Jeff wanted to be the first to escort me to a public dungeon, the Switch Club, Chicago's members-only dungeon. I thought the whole idea was smashing. We were half-popped when we got there, which was frowned upon at a dungeon. But we were there to observe, not to scene. The Switch Club was in a century-old brick building. Within a minute, a lively and gracious petticoated sissy maid stepped out of the front entrance to welcome us. The maid, decked in lace and satin, spoke with a feminine tone over a man's voice. It was one of the first times I had been in the presence of a cross-dresser.

Once inside, we passed through to the dungeon's main room with its high ceilings, mirrors on the walls, bondage tables, St. Anthony crosses for floggings and spanking bench. The first thing we saw was a three-hundred-pound woman naked and spread-eagle on a bondage table. It was a shocking sight! I had no qualms about others doing as they pleased, but public scening didn't appeal to me. I saw a power exchange as an emotional connection with another person, not necessarily something visible. After an hour we were finished. Neither of us particularly liked the Switch Club, so I chalked the night up to a case study in the BDSM sub-culture.

I couldn't wait to blindfold Jeff, put him in bondage then rifle through his toys. I was already dressed to scene so we did what came naturally back at his place. Our scening wasn't too intense that night, just a little light bondage. I tied him to the bed with leather cuffs and rope. I also covered his eyes with a sheepskin and leather blindfold and put nipple clamps on him. During sensation play, I rapped his Prince Albert with my riding crop and spanked, tickled and teased him. He was blindfolded so he never knew what sensation would come next–pain or pleasure. Pleasure could be lightly grazing his skin, kissing or whispering in his ear. After scening I slipped into my nightgown. The last image I had that night was Jeff wearing my torn fishnets, peacefully asleep on top of the covers. People in his circles would never guess such a kinky freak lived under his conservative corporate mettle.

Jeff woke up still elated and literally leapt about his apartment, wearing nothing but my ragged hosiery as he brewed coffee. "I'm going to wear these all day!" he said. He slid his Levi's over my fishnets and put on a v-neck and leather jacket, announcing he intended to ride his Harley in my stockings. My only regret was not leaving an extra pair for him in Chicago.

My next adventure, Byron, lived in southern California and flew planes long before he could legally drive a car. I was intrigued by his backstory. He was well-mannered and courteous in all our chats. I felt confident he respected me so I granted him the privilege of talking on the phone.

He seemed safe and genuinely took interest in me as a person.

Within a few days we spent all our free nights on the phone. His easiness made me feel as if he were an old friend. Bryon had experienced some intense lifestyle scening. He described crawling to greet his former mistress to lick the bottom of her shoes clean each time she walked in the door. This wasn't unusual behavior for a lot of subs. He loved being used in any way the domme felt was fitting. Byron didn't have a lot of limits outside the norm. He said no permanent marks and no drugs. He agreed to hop a flight and meet me in Indianapolis.

We locked eyes and sparks flew when he arrived. Byron's picture didn't do him justice. That night after a long talk on the porch, he said, "I know the perfect thing to relax you so you'll fall right asleep, Miss."

We went upstairs and he told me to lie on my down comforter and close my eyes. Then he began to lightly graze every bit of skin left accessible by my skirt and camisole. I felt completely calm.

"I could sit here all night and stroke you." he said. "You deserve only the best."

For the next hour Byron ran his hands over my body then I instructed him to kneel on the floor beside my bed. I sat up and leaned into him. We connected seamlessly and kissed for a few minutes. I was hungry for more but came to my senses. I had to make sure not to spoil Byron. I told him to go to bed and said I would knock on his door when it was time to wake up.

After breakfast the next day we set out to see my favorite places around the city. On the way to the Indianapolis Museum of Art, we talked about what D/s meant to each of us. I told him I saw a profound beauty in a pure power exchange. He said he got off on serving.

We walked, holding hands on the natural stone paths. The wooded landscape at the museum had perennial gardens of plants indigenous to Indiana and many sculptures from the Lilly family's art collection stood on display on the grounds. The expansive lawn in front of the Lilly Mansion had at its furthest reach a classical Greek marble sculpture called Three Graces. It depicted two bare-breasted, barefooted maidens adorning their lady with a crown of flowers.

"The girls are obviously submissive to a mistress," I said to Byron. "See? The maiden girls are barefoot and the lady has on sandals." I had never made a D/s connection before in art. After that, I noticed D/s all around me.

> Every woman should experience dommespace at least once. For me, it is a form of self-possession.

As we strolled the grounds, Byron emphasized that as his domme, I should not be afraid to perform acts that seemed extreme. He gave me permission to take him down as brutally as I could. I could kick, slap, bite, smack, yell or demand of him any humiliating behavior that came to mind. He told me to take my frustrations out on him and said it wasn't fun unless he felt completely stripped of control. The scene, his submitting and my taking control in a power exchange, everything had to be real.

"Remember, I can always use my safeword," Byron said, "but I never will."

Our D/s discussion was fascinating, considering how serenely we talked about acts that on the surface seemed violent. Our conversational tone suited the tranquil environment. We were planning an adventure that would give a sense of fulfillment to the other and an odd peace-odd because of the way it would come about. I had Byron's consent to act out my aggressions along with my fantasies. I had permission to lay it all on him. My mind whirred with the unlimited potential to do whatever I wanted.

Byron was a different type of submissive than Jeff. For Byron, D/s was primarily mental and this made him far more interesting and complex to me. This meant I could dominate Byron without using a physical object. I could do it with my mind. Jeff was a fetishist which meant he had an excessive attachment to and was aroused by objects. If it was weird and made of leather or steel, he wanted it. Jeff wasn't overly oriented toward service but in scene, he needed to feel the transfer of power to his domme to enjoy the experience.

After returning from our field trip, I anxiously began to take ownership of Byron.

"Down on your knees, boy," I commanded. "You are mine, now. Do you willingly give yourself to me?"

"Yes, Miss!" he said.

I was morphing into character and it seemed Byron was relieved to see me take charge.

"Strip, stand and get naked right now," I commanded. "Then take your clothes to your room, hang them up and report back to me immediately!"

"Yes, Miss!" With pep in his step, he dashed up the stairs then returned.

"Stand with your hands behind your neck and spread your legs."

Byron's nakedness seemed to kick in his submissive headspace. I walked circles around him, holding my riding crop and staring him up and down, savoring him. I ran the crop up and down his body, grazed my fingers across his silky chest hair then clenched his chin in my hand.

"You will give yourself completely to me," I said. "Am I clear?"

Byron became visibly aroused. As I drank in every inch of my new canvas, the power exchange began. I toyed the leather collar in front of his face.

"When I put this collar on you, it means I own you while you wear it," I said. "Is that what you want?"

He didn't hesitate to say, yes. I secured it to his neck with a small padlock and put the key on my sterling chain. I wanted him to always see that I held the key. I clipped a leash to the collar and gave it a soft tug, kissing Byron's forehead. I slipped deeper into dommespace.

Every woman should experience dommespace at least once. For me it is a form of self-possession. The creativity I channel makes me feel as if I'm composing and conducting a symphony. The subs are my obedient orchestra whom I direct and control. The world outside fades as my mind constructs our private concert hall. Ultimately I feel safe because I'm designing our playground.

"C'mon Byron. We're going for a little walk out into the garden," I said. "It's dark now and I have a privacy fence. You'll be fine."

I wanted to let him experience the warm spring air on his body, then I led him to my enclosed veranda which had blinds so he was hidden from view.

"Go ahead and touch yourself," I said. "It's okay. Continue to pleasure yourself while I get the rest of dinner together."

"Yes, Miss," Byron said.

"Oh, one thing Byron," I said. "You are not allowed to lose control. Are we clear? If you do, I am going to give you fifty hard strokes with my crop. You wouldn't like that, would you?"

"No, Miss. I would hate that," he said. "I'll do exactly as you order."

I kept my eye on him through the kitchen window. Sure enough, he was out there, doing just as I had directed. I thought, "How cerebral, bizarre and totally fun." Sex with other men no longer seemed memorable. Not that there was anything wrong with their lovemaking but it was just routine. This encounter I would remember my entire life. Dinner needed more time, so I opened two more beers and headed outside. I noticed Byron's collar was off-center, so I reached down to straighten it. Then something happened.

"I am sooooo sorry, Miss!" Byron exclaimed. "I didn't . . . I'm sorry. I don't know what happened! I promise, I didn't mean to!"

Byron's panic caught me by surprise. I surveyed the scene to see what was going on. To my amazement when I touched his collar, he had lost control, a highly unusual response for such an experienced sub.

"I'll punish you later," I said, sitting in the Adirondack chair next to him. "Right now, I want to talk about what just happened. Did you understand it?"

"No, Miss, I don't know why I did that." He was on the verge of tears. "I mean, this never happens."

"You climaxed the second I touched your collar, remember? I think you connected my hand on your collar to being owned. And isn't being owned what you crave most?"

"Yes, Miss. I need it," Byron said. "You're still going to punish me though, aren't you?"

His remark meant he was topping from the bottom. I gave him a thunk on the head with my knuckles.

"You'll be punished tomorrow. Tonight I want to enjoy you."

Byron sat at my feet on the floor in the dining room while I hand-fed him bites from my plate. I lingered my fingers in his mouth and allowed him little sips of drink from my glass. I was enjoying my sexy pet.

Once he had cleaned the dishes and the kitchen to my satisfaction, I told him to draw me a bath and then wait downstairs in the kneeling position. After bathing, I put on satin pajamas and went back down to the living room. Byron was waiting just as I wanted.

"Crawl over here," I said.

Byron immediately inched to my feet.

"Here's some lotion, pet. You know what to do."

Bryon's love of feet was one of the first things I'd learned about him during our chats. He rubbed lotion into my feet and legs for an eternity. Next, I demanded foot worship. He slowly and softly caressed my foot with both hands and kissed every inch of my leg from my knee to calf, then down to the bottoms of my feet. Every toe was passionately kissed and licked.

I was completely aroused. The rest of the night was spent making sure I was pleased and fully satisfied before bed. Byron was allowed the privilege of sleeping at the foot of my bed that night. I kept his leash in my hand as he dozed off.

> This was the most hardcore scene I had ever conducted. I was in dommespace the whole time and was able to let the guilt go. Dommespace was pure freedom.

The morning sun shone brightly through the east window of the master bedroom as I awoke.

"Get up, my pet," I said. "It'll soon be time for your punishment. Are you excited?"

"No, Miss," Byron said in full character. "I hate punishment. I'm sorry, Miss."

"Don't worry," I said. "It will hurt a lot but it won't last long. It's just fifty strokes as hard as I can land them on your bare ass. What kind of domme would I be if I didn't punish you?"

"Not a very good one, Miss. I deserve it for disobeying you even if I couldn't help it."

"Go make me some coffee while I get dressed," I said. "Then I want you to remove your collar and take a quick shower and shave. When you finish, don't get dressed. Report to me naked."

When Byron returned, I locked his collar and told him to lie across the edge of my bed and wait for his punishment. I left him waiting for about fifteen minutes, knowing that time spent in anticipation of pleasure and fearing pain would take him right back to subspace.

Crop in hand, I returned. "You're to count off each stroke and say, thank you, Miss, for making me a better sub, fifty times. You get zero space between strikes. This is punishment, got it? You should have never let yourself go like that last night without permission. You disobeyed me. Now this is going to hurt."

By the time he had counted to twenty, Byron had a hard time thanking me. I administered his correction quickly and with as much force as possible. When the punishment was over, I rubbed his red, welted behind with lotion. I didn't have to but I wanted to be nice. Plus it was a good scene.

That night, I had something I'd never tried before in mind for Byron. I was going to take him down. At dusk I made Byron wait naked in a kneeling position with his legs folded under him and his hands clasped behind his back. I went upstairs to get into a full-blown dominatrix costume. I laid out my stockings, waist-cincher with garters, push-up bra, thigh-high boots with five-inch platform heels and a sexy low-cut blazer that hit me about mid-leg. I put on heavier eye makeup, lipstick and Coco Chanel perfume. I felt fantastic.

I was sure Byron could hear my boots on the staircase.

When I rounded the corner and saw him kneeling, he was already aroused.

"Crawl over here, slave, and lick my boots!" I said.

He seemed eager to obey. I clipped the leash to his collar then led him to my vintage sofa and shoved his head into the cushion. Then I held him in place with my knee in his back and reached for my toy bag under the sofa. Taking out a spandex hood, I pulled it down over his head.

"You're mine, bitch!" I shouted. "You're going to see what it's like to be used."

I got a rope from the bag and tied his hands in a cuff knot, securing them to the wrought iron on the sofa. Once he was bound, a rabbit fur mitt with little spikes concealed in one side of the pelt made him start writhing. I stroked him first with the soft side then dragged the spikes across his ass, repeating the sequence several times, followed by a hard whack with a cherry wood paddle. The spandex hood muffled his moans as I peppered soft hits with hard smacks, not stopping until the capillaries came to the surface of his skin.

This was the most hardcore scene I had ever conducted and it was stretching my boundaries of comfort. Relieved I couldn't see his face, part of me loved it while at the same time, I felt guilty and insecure. I had never inflicted so much pain on anyone but despite my serious misgivings, I was in dommespace the whole time and was able to let the guilt go. Dommespace was pure freedom.

When I pulled the hood off, he squinted and looked

dumfounded by what had just happened. Pain initiated the body's natural fight or flight response with a rush of epinephrine and endorphins that in turn could make the sub feel as if he was flying or out-of-body. Afterward the sub might even be incoherent. I was worried that I had been too rough.

"That was great, Miss! I was terrified, thinking what was next," Byron said. "That's exactly what I needed!"

Byron didn't leave the following day as he had originally planned. We remained in a blissful state of domme space and subspace for our entire five days together.

Being the right domme was important for my next sub, Jonathan, because he was a novice. An elite trained Army Ranger with dreamy looks, an open mind and an interest in D/s, he was a hard man to resist. However, I knew he was inexperienced and it would be best to keep our sexual connection to a minimum, if at all. D/s starts in the mind and letting him have me physically was not the right path. Jonathan needed to learn the fundamentals. My goal was to make it a peak experience for both of us. It was difficult to plan that in advance because creating a peak experience while immersed in sub and dommespace was often spontaneous and different for each scene. Jonathan arrived, wearing aviator sunglasses and luggage in hand. I showed him to his room to get settled. Later as we sat on the porch, I asked him what it was like to be a ranger.

"I'm fascinated by a man in uniform," I said.

He told me he was switching agencies and was going to be a DEA agent.

"You're going to bust people for pot?"

"No, Miss," he said. Jonathan was prepared to address me properly. "I would help stop international drug trade."

Once we were a little more used to each other, I asked about his fetish.

"Do you know much about queening, Miss?" he asked.

I had heard of queening but was shocked a novice would bring it up. In queening the sub was placed in bondage, sometimes strict bondage such as mummification, so the queen could use his face and mouth to pleasure herself.

"Yes, Miss," Jonathan said. "I've been dreaming of doing that to you."

"Well, you're going to be dreaming a long time, Jonathan," I said. "You have not earned that from me, have you?"

"I want to earn that, Miss," he said. "Do you think that's possible?"

"We'll see how well you perform tonight in the scene I have planned for you," I said.

Still I had no idea what I was going to do with Jonathan. I was trying to wrap my head around his psychology.

"Want another beer?" I asked.

"That would be great, Miss."

"Then what are you waiting for?" I raised my voice. "You're the sub! Get up and get me a beer!"

"Yes, Miss." He looked embarrassed.

When Jonathan returned, I took a serious tone with him.

"Look, you drove a long way to learn about D/s," I

said. "Do you trust me? Do you still want to go forward with this?"

"I would do anything for you right now, Miss," Jonathan said.

I left the porch and returned with my riding crop, leather collar and padlock. I showed Jonathan the collar and asked if he knew what it meant. He said he did. To be sure, I explained the symbolism and asked if he wanted to wear the collar. By then I had him kneeling in my living room.

"Yes, Miss. I came here to wear your collar. That's what I want."

"How does it feel, Jonathan?" I asked. "Are you comfortable?"

"I like it, Miss," he said softly.

"Good, I think you may make a fine pet for me," I told him. " Now I'm going to clip this leash to your collar and we're going to go for a little walk around the house."

Jonathan crawled like a dog through the rooms then I sat in a chair with him at my feet and taught him foot worship.

"You are not allowed to put your hands anywhere above my knee," I said. "You haven't earned that."

"I understand, Miss," he said. "I like this a lot."

For the next hour he worshipped my feet as I planned what to do with my new toy. My libido was sky high. I knew better than to have another beer. It was getting late when it finally came to me how to make Jonathan click.

"You have a choice where to sleep tonight," I said. "You may take the guest room or you can sleep on the floor chained and padlocked to the foot of my bed."

"Chained to the foot of your bed?" Jonathan obviously didn't like his choices. "Really, Miss?"

I led Jonathan upstairs and ordered him to strip. Within seconds he stood before me, wearing only his collar. I laid a comforter and pillow on the floor at the foot of the bed and told him to lie down then cuffed his ankle to the bedpost and put the keys on the chain around my neck.

"Your safeword is black," I said, leaving the room.

In the bathroom, I put on a white silk nightgown and looked myself over in the mirror before returning to the bedroom. As soon as I stood over him with one foot on either side of his torso, he reached for my leg.

"How dare you!" I shouted. "Did I say you could touch me, Jonathan?"

I reached down and lightly slapped his face, letting him see my cleavage.

"You are never to touch your domme without permission. Am I clear?"

"Yes, Miss," he said. "Sorry, Miss."

I didn't want to be cruel so I gave in a bit. "You can worship my legs now but only as far as my knee."

He caressed each leg while trying to catch a glimpse up my gown.

"You know I have nothing on under my nightgown, don't you?"

"Yes, Miss. I can tell."

"How would you like for me to take it off and stand over you, naked right now?"

"I want you to do that more than anything right now, Miss."

"Okay, then, Jonathan, I will. But first I have another little present for you."

I placed cuffs on his wrists, locked them together and attached the cuffs to the bedpost. Both wrists and one ankle were chained to the bed.

"There's one more thing I want to do before taking this nightgown off." I paused. "You're going to wear a blindfold."

I put the blindfold on him and left the room again for several minutes to apply some scented lotion, leaving him to simmer. A few minutes later I returned and stood over him again. Leaning over I ran my hands up and down his body. Then I slipped the nightgown over my head and dropped it on his chest. He gasped.

"Please, Miss, please!" he said. "Please let me see you."

"What kind of domme would I be if I let you have everything you wanted?" I said. "I don't deserve a spoiled sub, do I?"

"No, Miss. You don't." His voice shook. "What do I have to do?"

"You need to learn to be the very best sub you can be for me. Think about that while I crawl into my nice cozy bed and pleasure myself."

I slipped between the sheets and began making moaning sounds. Before I could reach a fake orgasm, he screamed, "Black! Black! Black!"

I got up, put my robe on, turned on the lights and removed his bondage. Scene over.

Jonathan, an elite soldier trained to be a prisoner of war, was embarrassed that he had safeworded. He spent the night in the guest room and I kissed him before saying goodbye the next day.

ChapterFive

Christina, a cute Japanese-American girl in her early twenties who worked at a nearby Starbucks, answered an ad for a roommate I'd placed. I needed a little extra for my living expenses. Christina turned out to be much more than just a tenant. Shortly after she moved in, she revealed she'd had a vision that told her to move to a particular house. "I recognized the bedroom with yellow walls and red velvet drapes. I also saw an herb garden," she said. "Your house is the exact match and that's why I moved here."

Since I was a firm believer in harbingers and omens, I had no doubt she was telling the truth. This was another one of the coincidences that were beginning to show up in my life more frequently. Then Christina went further to say she'd answered my ad to set me up in business!

When Christina first moved in, I mentioned I dated a lot and gave the impression I saw a few different men more or less platonically. Since she spent days at a time at her boyfriend's house, I wasn't too worried about her walking in on any D/s activities. One day Christina plopped herself down on the porch and confessed something personal. I was dumbfounded.

"I think I'm dominating my boyfriend," she said. "Can we talk about it?"

Initially, I thought Christina was trying to get me to tell her about my secret kinky life because she'd looked in the leather satchel of toys I kept in my closet.

"What makes you think you're dominating your boyfriend?"

"I tell him what to wear and eat everyday. I say when and where we have sex and I usually hold him down. He never gets a release unless I say so. Sometimes I make him go for more than a week."

I hadn't realized Christina was such a siren. She was naturally stunning and it didn't take much make-up to transform her into a provocative woman. Later on, she admitted sneaking into my room and sifting through the toy bag. She must have been keen to learn more about my clandestine sex life, but I would have never guessed Christina was a closeted dominatrix.

During her childhood she used her allowance to pay boys in the neighborhood to let her tie them with rope, doll them up and spank them. Her confession was bizarre but believable. It sounded as if she had the ability to convince a guy to do anything. I laughed, imagining her a little playground dominatrix, sending boys crying on their bikes to tell their moms.

One day she asked, "Mely, what would you think if I became an escort?"

Doing something like that had never crossed my mind. Christina was grown up and could do whatever she wanted. She didn't need my approval.

"The question is not what I think, Christina, but what you would think of yourself?" I said.

She had already interviewed with an agency she called legit. At the time I was unaware such agencies even existed, let alone how a girl like Christina would locate one. I made her promise not to give out my address to her employer or clients and she swore she wouldn't bring anything remotely close to my front door. Fortunately, she only ended up working there for a week.

After Christina had been living in my house for a while, I met my first male dominant online. Antonio had recently relocated from the South to Indianapolis to take over a large transportation company. Our friendship began by just taking walks together after work. He told me about living with two female subs in his last place. His perspective was mesmerizing. Antonio became restless after moving to Indianapolis and craved more spice in his life. We were perfect pals but shared no relationship alchemy beyond our bizarre budding friendship.

One day he admitted to not being able to keep his apartment clean and I suggested he move into my house for the same rent as his apartment. I guaranteed he would come home to a clean house because I couldn't stand it any other way. Antonio accepted the invitation and moved in. Christina's reaction was to keep her distance the same way a cat treats a new dog in the house. In return, Antonio didn't trust her one bit either.

> " I could hear the loud crack of her paddle all the way down the corridor, the sound of hardwood smacking bare ass and echoing past dozens of doors. I was convinced our little enterprise would land us in jail.

Christina demanded to be called Mistress Claudia as soon as she scheduled her first D/s session with a paying client. She booked from a classified ad she ran. She asked me to run security for her that evening, probably already counting on me to tag along with her.

"Do you even know what you're going to wear?" I asked. "What toys are you going to use?"

She appeared to have no game plan for the night. "Well, I thought you would lend me your thigh-high boots, your cuffs and your crop," she said. I could see she was going to take what she needed whether I consented or not.

"Antonio, come downstairs please," I shouted. "We need to talk!"

I laid out what Mistress Claudia had in mind for that night and asked Antonio if he would come along. She was going on the job with or without me and I felt compelled to make sure she was protected.

"Oh, boy! An adventure! I'm in!" Antonio declared.

An hour later we were driving north in my Altima toward her sub's house, discussing on the way every conceivable contingency plan in case something shady went down. Mistress Claudia had our phone numbers on speed dial and we synchronized our watches. She agreed to return to the car in no more than an hour or she could expect us to go in to get her. We sent Claudia off and parked around the corner to wait.

"I wonder what she's doing in there?" we both said at the same time.

The seconds ticked slowly by in the agonizing stillness. Antonio and I passed the time reading recipes from a *Bon Appétit* magazine I had in the car. Thank god, Claudia was back right on cue. She peeled off fifty dollars from a wad of cash and handed them to me. Antonio refused payment. He was in it purely for the sport. We were giddy all the way home about pulling off our first caper.

Next thing I knew, Mistress Claudia had a busy calendar. She stopped making house calls and started meeting clients in fancy rooms at upscale hotels. Claudia was completely entrenched in living out her fantasy as a full-time domme and asked me to take on the role of her madame. Being a professional madame didn't sit right with me but Claudia was a tiny thing and my conscience wouldn't allow me to send her out into the night alone. The world was filled with sociopaths and we never knew who was at the other end of the line, requesting her services. She could have been beaten, raped or robbed.

I agreed once again to be her security but insisted on handling the upfront details with her clients. I wasn't going to be able to stop Claudia and part of me didn't want to, so screening guys would allow me to weed out potential danger. Yet, no matter how hard I tried to legitimize being her madame in my mind, I still felt uneasy. Living on the edge gave me the unsettled feeling we might get busted. In a way we were addicted to scening because doing something that freaking out-of-the-box felt unbelievably liberating. It was like a drug. The fact was, I was an account executive by day and a madame for a dominatrix at dusk.

We booked three or four clients spaced about ninety minutes apart on the evenings she took sessions. I met the clients in their rooms first to explain the rules and take their cash. I always wore a conservative black business suit and boots. Very professional. I laid low by the elevators to make sure everything was kosher and no one knocked on Claudia's door. I could hear the loud crack of her paddle all the way down the corridor, the sound of hardwood smacking bare ass and echoing past dozens of doors. I was always worried our little enterprise would land us in jail.

As it turned out, the innocent little girl whose hair bounced as she walked up my front walk a few months earlier was a hard-core sadist. She was also drop-dead gorgeous as a domme and men couldn't resist her. Being a business-minded internaut, I created an online persona for Mistress Claudia and started handling her bookings online. One of my two telephone landlines was also dedicated to the business. It became apparent that Indy had a long pent-up market for professional domination and I started to grow more relaxed in my role as madame and protector of Mistress Claudia.

One day I flirted with a local handsome boy-next-door type named Paul. I mentioned our little enterprise and he called for a session. I was envious of Mistress Claudia for getting all the action. After his session, Claudia told me she didn't think it went well and the only explanation she could give was that they didn't connect mentally–essential for a successful session. Under the guise of customer follow-up, I called and asked him if he would meet me for a drink. Sipping gin and tonic, he sheepishly admitted what had gone wrong.

"Honestly, I really wanted it to be you behind the door," he said.

Paul said he preferred my age, experience and my looks to Mistress Claudia's younger, more exotic flavor. He asked if I would be available. I was hot for this guy and with little delay agreed to take his session at the customary fee. The fear of someone hearing me at the hotel was worrisome so I invited him to session at my house instead. We agreed to meet the next evening.

"Please, kneel right here," I said when he arrived. "Do you have your tribute for me?"

I asked him to put the cash in his mouth and plucked the bills from between his lips. My tribute presentation ritual began that evening.

"You may now kiss my boots to thank me for my attention."

"Thank you, Miss," Paul said, lowering his face to the floor.

I led Paul to the extra room upstairs. My first order of business was Paul's inspection.

"Strip right now so I can appraise my property," I said.

Paul was lean, well-built and didn't have tattoos. I told him to kneel for the collar and locked it on his neck.

"When you're in this room with me, I am in charge. Your safeword is black. Use the word if you feel in danger of physical or psychological harm. Are you clear on that?"

Paul was an experienced sub and had much more time in his role than I did as a domme. I knew there was no way he would safeword. I blindfolded him and told him to stand by the bed as I removed my skirt, leaving my blazer on, to reveal the garters attached to my bustier and expose five inches of thigh. After lighting a candle, I ran my crop up and down his body and spanked his ass lightly a few times.

"I see Mistress Claudia's marks on you from last night. If you dare move, I will strike you just as hard."

He posed like a soldier. I then removed a roll of Saran Wrap from the closet.

"Keep your hands at your side and remain absolutely still," I said.

I wrapped the plastic around his ankles and worked up his legs. Before long, his arms were secured to his torso. I wound the sheeting until I had him packaged in two transparent layers all the way up to his neck. Paul was incapable of moving any part of his body except his feet and head. I tipped him backward onto the bed.

Medical scissors prevented me nicking him as I carefully cut the plastic away from his nipples and his erection. I was eager to play with my mummified man. I removed the blindfold.

"Thank you, Miss, for taking ownership of me," he said. "I am yours to do with as you please."

"Now that you've seen me," I said, "I'm going to replace your blindfold. Hold my image in your mind while I take your body on a journey."

One at a time I slowly flicked, rubbed and tweaked his nipples. He gasped and groaned. I reached for the candle, held it above him, letting it trickle drop by drop onto his nipples until they were plastered in wax. Then I lightly stroked his face with the back of my hand.

"You please me, pet. Do you want more of my love?"

"Yes, Miss."

I slapped his erection gingerly with my crop, gauging his pain response by his moans. Swatting him harder several more times, I increased then decreased the force of each stroke. Then I picked up the candle again and slowly covered his privates with wax.

"Now that you're fully encased in wax and plastic, I have a treat for you."

I put a sheet across his body and straddled him as he attempted to writhe under my weight. I leaned forward, my face inches from his, and removed the blindfold. Nuzzling his neck so he could inhale my perfume, I ever so softly breathed in his ear, "You are a fine play thing, Paul. I enjoy you very much." Then I stretched out on top of him for several minutes.

Afterward, I slowly cut him from bondage. He began to slip out of sub space as the oxygen in the room cooled his exposed skin. I put my skirt back on and left the room, pleased with the scene. Before Paul left, he knelt to kiss my feet and thanked me once more. I hugged him at the door and as we said our goodbyes, I was thrilled to have been paid for something I would have done for free. My pro domme cherry was popped.

As work became more and more lucrative, we moved all of our sessions from the hotel to my house. Even through the highs of running a scandalous small business, I was terrified of people's perceptions. I worried about everything: paying the bills, safety, and the law. Then one day I got an idea that would change everything. My earnings would go toward a complete overhaul of the basement from a dingy, unfinished storage space to a full-on D/s dungeon. We were going underground!

> " Wearing four-inch shiny platform boots and a coat straight out of The Matrix, I walked into the party as if I owned it. In D/s, my condition was known as domme-itis.

On demolition day I took a hammer to the plasterboard ceiling covering the rafters, causing decades of dust and debris to rain down. Thick cobwebs and dead bugs fell from the ceiling joists along with chunks of plasterboard painted a sickening institution green color. A crowbar did the trick to pry off the faux wood paneling and two-by-fours attaching it to the basement walls. With the fake ceiling and walls in a dumpster, I had a blank canvas downstairs. Then I posted an announcement online, calling for submissives to help complete the dungeon.

Slave Trevor was the first to show up. I came home from the office one day to find him doing housework. Mistress Claudia had made him scrub the bathroom top to bottom.

"Stand up and present yourself, slave!" Claudia ordered. "Is my bathroom ready for inspection, you insignificant worm?"

"Yes, Mistress, it is," Trevor answered nervously. "I cleaned everything just as you asked."

Claudia inspected the toilet and shower and in less than two minutes found several minor flaws with the cleaning. Signs of Trevor's insolence infuriated her.

"Strip, now!" she said.

Trevor appeared happy to set the scrub brush down and remove his clothing and rubber gloves. Mistress Claudia grabbed one of my training collars and securely padlocked it around his neck.

"Since you say the bathroom is perfectly clean and sanitized, then you won't mind licking every inch of the toilet inside and out, will you?" she said.

"No, Mistress. I won't mind."

I watched in disbelief as she forced him down on all fours and shoved his head toward the toilet.

"Next time you say you want to serve over here, you better act like it," she said.

Claudia put her heel into his back, forcing Trevor to lick the entire toilet. It was one of the most intense scenes I had ever witnessed. From then on, Trevor was Claudia's. He reported to her on days he didn't wait tables. She stripped him naked and left him alone in the dungeon to do solitary labor. Trevor's immediate future was removing paint from the exposed concrete walls. He scraped and swept paint chips for days on end.

Antonio and I were playing Scrabble and drinking wine one night when Claudia allowed Trevor to come up from his dungeon drudgery and shower. After he was clean, she let him lie under her boots while she sat on the sofa. She flogged him with deliberate laziness. Slave Trevor was on cloud nine any time Claudia paid him even the smallest amount of notice. He was even happier when others were in the room to witness him in his most pathetic state. Trevor didn't really yearn for servitude, rather he was starved for any sort of attention–especially negative.

After the basement was cleaned and the walls tuck-pointed, I had to decide where bondage chains should be placed and then have twenty eyebolts set directly into the masonry. Another sub, Ishmael, who was an electrical project manager volunteered to do the lighting. He wasn't submissive in the strictest sense but had a life-long spanking fetish and was willing to wire my new studio for the price of being behind the scenes of Dungeon Arts.

Years earlier I'd bought a 1930's gothic wrought-iron and stained-glass light fixture that seemed destined to be the main architectural element. Ishmael also insisted a spotlight be installed at the far end of the dungeon where he envisioned it highlighting a lone chair used solely for OTK (over-the-knee) spankings.

With the dungeon under construction, I quit my corporate job in preparation for my new profession. In the middle of the construction, Claudia brought home bad news for me. She informed me that she was moving to the east coast to follow her boyfriend to a new job he landed. I was going to have to go it alone.

My first day at home I went downstairs to transform the sunroom from a corporate home office to the workspace of a professional dominatrix. After pulling open every drawer of the filing cabinet, I pitched a tree's worth of documents into a trash can. My computer desk sat next to an oak bookshelf loaded with small items which I removed so I could dust and reorganize. As I placed a picture of my grandmother on the desk, I spied something on top of the bookshelf and retrieved a Rider-Waite tarot deck I'd purchased at a yard sale as a Halloween prop.

An odd chill ran through me as I touched the cards. I turned to toss them in the trash but they slid out of the box onto the carpet so I had to gather them up before tossing them. The next morning when I sat at my desk to conference with the graphic designer building my Dungeon Arts website, I saw a loose tarot card leaning against the chair leg. It turned out to be three cards stuck together, the Knight of Wands, the Queen of Wands and the Knight of Cups.

Tarot was something I had never given much thought but the three cards improbably stuck together could only be an important sign. Intrigued, I laid them out to study. Each pictured a regal character on a vivid blue background. The Knight of Wands, representing alienation, rode a horse rearing to the west. He wore armor under a yellow cloak and a helmet with a large red feather. In his right hand he

KNIGHT of WANDS.
Alienation

QUEEN of WANDS.
A good harvest

KNIGHT of CUPS.
A fortunate visit

held a staff. The Queen of Wands held a similar staff in her right hand and a sunflower in her left. She symbolized a good harvest. Red-haired and fair-skinned, she sat on a throne in a yellow gown and modest crown with a black cat at her feet. The Knight of Cups foresaw a fortunate visit. He rode a white horse and was preparing to cross a river. Wearing armor, he was forthright and carried a gold chalice.

I turned to my computer to confirm my impressions. Two of the cards clicked with me immediately. The Knight of Wands was Alan and the Queen of Wands represented me. Alan had ridden into my life, charging into my psyche and taking over my body. Our relationship was fiery like the knight. He had taught me D/s. As for me, I could see sunflowers depicted in the Queen's card, blooming through my sunroom windows. My black cat Sophie was at my feet.

One evening Antonio and I were drinking beers on the front porch when I found a small ad for a fetish event on October 31, at Fountain Square Theater. Knowing a fetish party was coming up made me even more determined to meet my construction deadline. I was going to that party as a domme with her own dungeon and nothing was going to stop me.

I thought I was something. I'm actually embarrassed about the way I talked back then, but in retrospect my boisterous tone helped hammer home my ambitious plans and ideas. Wearing four-inch shiny platform boots and a coat straight out of The Matrix, I walked into the fetish party as if I owned it. Scouting the crowd, I saw subs turn their gaze elsewhere to avoid making eye contact with me. Even though I had not accomplished much else other than renovating a basement, I thought I was a messiah. In D/s, my condition was called domme-itis.

The fetish party had a small vendor area where I bought a delightful leather flogger with a hand-carved penis handle. Next to it was an impressive stainless steel whipping cross for sale. I fantasized about flogging a boy tied up to it. If I owned it, the cross would be the signature piece to tie the dungeon together. Later that evening, I talked to the artist, Gil, who had made the cross.

I had just transformed my basement into a killer gothic dungeon space, and needed furniture. Plus our new business, Dungeon Arts, was picking up a serious following around town. Gil seemed enthralled less with the dungeon and more about me blossoming into a full-time professional dominatrix. Turns out, he was looking for his own sustainable kinky situation. I expounded on some specifics about what went down at my house. Gil wanted in. A few days later, Gil sold me the cross for the cost of materials.

Gil moved into my house for a while. He was a hard-core latex fetishist and bondage aficionado who spent every spare cent on custom European house latex costumes and laboriously studied and planned his outfits to perfection. His evening hobby was dressing up as a woman in elaborate latex costumes and appearing on webcam for the pleasure of an online audience. For his efforts at Dungeon Arts, I provided him an allowance to appear as the latex pet in my dungeon. Part of his job description was to set a proper example when we trained new submissives.

Sometimes Gil was instructed to lap milk from a bowl in a demonstration of depersonalization, which meant turning a submissive into a machine, object or animal. For a while I was into forcing subs to act like cats, cleaning themselves with their tongues and purring at my feet.

Antonio, Gil and I had a computer bank in my sunroom which wrapped around the side of my house where we were visible to passersby, but no one seemed to notice the feminized latex freak sometimes on full display. As far as we were concerned, the more bizarre the better. My new age reading taught that the only way to protect oneself from forces of darkness was to act in the full light of day where the forces of darkness were benign.

Within a few months of the latex kitten moving in with our little family, I envisioned myself as a femme domme version of Hugh Hefner and started lounging around at night in satin pajamas.

It took Gil two full hours to put on his costumes and apply detailed make-up that peered through the eyeholes of his masks. He was meticulous about his latex. Cleaning it was tedious but to Gil, it was a ritual. Each time the latex was washed, he hung it to drip dry and then lightly dusted it with powder on the inside. Gil had one chance to slip into the latex and if he had skimmed on the dusting, it was a pain to put on.

Once in his full cat suit, the outside was dull and dusty from the talc. More than one person had to help him hand-polish his latex with the contents of a one hundred dollar bottle of lubricant from Germany, formulated not to chemically interact with the fabric. If one dared shine latex with petroleum-based mineral oil, it would disintegrate.

I got a little bored keeping my latex kitten inside because I thought him far too fabulous not to be shared with the world. I longed to get him out into the light of day and sunshine. The fact that I also wanted some D/s marketing visuals gave me an idea. A photo shoot would serve my purposes and I knew just the guy to snap the pictures–Chris Gustafson, a talented fetish photographer from Detroit. Next, I needed to find a model with more sizzle than I possessed to put in front of the lens alongside my smoking hot latex pet.

Chapter Six

Antonio suffered from an addiction to strippers. In his quest for amusement in the sordid underworld of the bizarre, he spent several nights a week sipping bourbon at High Jinx. Antonio frequently wife-shopped at that point in his life, but because he was raised by a colorful Spanish-born matriarch he worshipped, the mother of his children could only be a devout Catholic–not an exotic dancer. He never cared for the girls after a couple of drinks and lap dances.

I told Antonio about my plan to bring the kink photographer to Indy and Antonio said he knew where I might find a subject, insisting that we attend the High Jinx upcoming monthly fetish night. I was model shopping and needed a unique, fetish-friendly beauty for the shoot. After getting settled at a table by the stage, we ordered drinks. An odor of cigarettes, tanning bed lotion and perfume permeated the stale air. I was already bored before the show began but promised to keep an open mind.

"Darling, if you see someone you like, let me know and I'll help seal a deal," he promised.

Within a few minutes the DJ cued up Depeche Mode's "Master and Servant" as a gorgeous, willowy girl self-consciously took the stage. She had long black hair and wore an oversized men's button-down shirt and black thigh-high stockings. Classic black stilettos with ankle-straps notched her look up to an uncommon level of good taste. I definitely liked the aura she exuded even if she did seem ever-so-slightly less than confident. Maybe the evening wouldn't be so dismal after all.

The wispy twenty-something kept my unflinching attention as she began to writhe and slowly unbutton the starched white oxford. Opening the shirt one button at a time, she revealed her nearly nude body wrapped in intricate Japanese rope bondage known as Shibari, originally a martial arts bondage. In the subculture of BDSM, Shibari means to tie. Her master had tied a harness accentuating her small breasts and flawless pale skin. Each knot was perfect and the symmetry precisely balanced. If suspension rigging had been set up on the stage, she could have been snugly hoisted by the Shibari. The girl wasn't as curvy or sexy as the other girls but possessed a unique appeal and haunting good looks.

Antonio and I sipped cocktails as the lyrics by Depeche Mode blared and I contemplated my new role as both a dominatrix and businesswoman. The sexy lyrics made me feel powerful. The idea of one day orchestrating a kink scene in Indy turned me on. When the dancer's set ended, I approached her.

"Your performance was lovely. Can we talk?"

The girl said she needed to ask her master first. I watched her slide in next to the strawberry blond-haired gentleman. With his long silky hair, he looked more like a well-groomed hippie than a traditional master. A few minutes later, they joined us.

"I'm Master Scott and this is my slave, Sydney," he said.

Expecting the night to be little more than hollow wannabe kinky performances, I was dumbfounded that within twenty minutes I'd found a real master and servant. Antonio sat back with a knowing grin on his face.

"Sydney's rope work is exquisite," I said.

"Shibari is a passion of mine."

"It's obvious! Do you have professional photographs of your slave in bondage?"

He said he hadn't catalogued any pictures of his pet at which point I told him about Chris Gustafson and asked if he would like to have his slave photographed in my gothic dungeon. Master Scott excused himself to speak privately with Sydney again. A few minutes later they returned and he agreed the opportunity was worth exploring. I suggested we meet the following Sunday in my home to discuss the details in the light of day.

I planned a semi-formal tea for my guests. When they arrived, I showed them around the house and poured Earl Grey from Grandma's teapot then led them downstairs to see my newly minted dungeon. Master Scott was on board as soon as he saw the space and Sydney consented. We returned to the dining room to hammer out details. Master Scott put the date on their calendar.

> "Her electric blue ponytail swung from her black latex hood. Only her eyes and lips in heavy make-up, false eyelashes and lipstick were revealed.

Then Sydney surprised me with a question. "What would you think of me being your apprentice?" she asked.

With Mistress Claudia living on the east coast, I conducted all the sessions and did not particularly like the work load. I preferred playing with my hand-picked lifestyle subs to conducting pro sessions for money. I jumped at her idea quickly. With a beautiful younger domme taking care of the dungeon maintenance and the clients, I could fully concentrate on what I loved most—marketing, playing madame and scening with friends I adored.

Sydney decided her scene name would be Lady Liza and we made plans to begin her training the following week. She was to assist in sessions for several weeks until she was ready to conduct them on her own. I agreed to pay her fifty dollars a session while she learned.

The photographer Chris arrived early on the scheduled Saturday morning, loaded with lights, tripods, several lenses and cameras. He set up his equipment within a couple hours and we were ready for the shoot by noon. Gil had awakened early that morning to spend the time necessary to get into his feminized latex and make-up. When Gil was out of character, he was male, but getting dolled up transformed him to her. Being photographed in her sleek latex suit, tightly cinched waist and big artificial breasts was a huge turn-on for my vain pet.

Master Scott, Sydney and Gil spent the entire afternoon in the dungeon with Chris, capturing intense imagery of the bondage and sensual domination. I stayed out of the way upstairs, knowing too many people could disrupt the energy of the power exchange. We planned to take a few simple portraits of me later in the evening. Besides, I was never quite at ease being photographed in scene anyway, preferring to market myself with classic portraiture.

After the day's shoot, everyone gathered on the front porch to digest the photos. Chris had captured emotional photos of Sydney chained, tied and ball-gagged, her face intense with pain and pleasure. Other pictures showed Scott by her side, lovingly dominating her in scene. We were all elated with the results, especially Chris. At that time it was some of his best work.

By the end of the day, Chris had developed a major crush on Sydney and couldn't get enough of her in front of his lens. He was hungry to shoot her again. Their relationship continued after that day with Sydney going up to Detroit for some one-on-one photography sessions with Chris.

I had a brilliant idea for a second shoot but had not been able to get Gil to consent, so I took advantage of the adrenaline that night on the front porch. I told Chris I wanted to produce a photograph that made a cutting statement about society and tolerance.

"I'm trying to talk Gil into wearing his latex outdoors so I can walk him as a pet on the Monon Trail."

The Monon was an asphalt rail trail running through Indy that was used daily by thousands of joggers, walkers and bicyclists. I explained Gil would be wearing more clothing than any cyclist or runner and I planned to wear slacks and a long jacket. It would be tasteful and fun.

"Besides, sometimes you see parents walking their kids on leashes and I'm curious to see if people will judge us for our choice of fabric," I said.

Chris loved the idea but Gil shifted uneasily in his seat. We reassured him that he would be disguised in his cat suit and a production crew would be there to set the scene. We would be artists doing something edgy!

"You need to trust us on this," I said. "My role as your domme is to push your edge and take you past what you think are your limits."

Latex kitten signed a model release on the spot and the shoot was scheduled three weeks later. Master Scott and Sydney wanted to come along and I was happy to have

Chris Gustafson, photographer

them join the group. I was nervous about the envelope we were going to push in our Midwest city and figured the more people on the adventure, the better.

On the day of the Monon Trail shoot, our entourage loaded into the Altima to embark on our next caper. I was juiced up but still anxious, not knowing how we would be received by the public. I noticed we needed fuel so without warning, I pulled into a gas station to get a couple shots of my extraordinary creature doing something ordinary. I wanted images of latex kitten pumping gas. I bribed the attendant with a twenty to let us spend some time shooting at the pumps. Then I coaxed Gil out of the car, instructing her how to hold the pump as Chris shot some images. Her electric blue ponytail swung from her black latex hood. Only her eyes and lips in heavy make-up, false eyelashes and lipstick were revealed. She was as stealth as cat woman.

I knew the best possible place to pull off the Monon Trail shoot without judgment was in Broad Ripple, known for its hip boutiques, restaurants, artists and open-minded people. We chose a section of the trail directly behind the Indianapolis Art Center with its fabulous industrial design as the backdrop for our photographs. The old Art Center building had been torn down and reinvented by Indiana-born architect Michael Graves in the mid-nineties. We parked close by and piled out of the car. People stared at us but did not react. Right away a father and son approached.

"Can my little boy meet Spider-Man?" he asked.

The movie *Spider-Man* was released the previous week to rave reviews.

"Sure your son can meet my friend, but it's spider-woman," I said.

The little boy seemed to have a larger-than-life experience on that warm spring afternoon.

"You caught one!" an older gentleman called out as I led latex kitten on the trail.

Other people we met on the trail spontaneously applauded our antics and their reception was heartwarming

ChapterSeven

A Chicago real estate developer of means was one of my first regular clients. Princess William was up for anything, no matter how crazy. He was married, a freak who had to have an outlet to express his bizarre brain, specifically with dommes who were professional and would not cross the sex line. He had a foot fetish and had served dommes' feet from coast-to-coast.

One day he told me about an extreme blackmail fantasy he wanted to explore. Financial domination was practiced by a domme whose sole purpose was to monetarily drain her sub, often through blackmail. In the most extreme cases, the domme might have the sub open one charge account after another until he couldn't get any more credit. Subs became addicted, perhaps in a way similar to a gambling addiction, but with sexual humiliation. Blackmail was a dangerous game and I didn't like it, but after a full year of working with Princess, I agreed.

I later wrote about it on my online forum in response to a member asking for advice about blackmail. This sub had found a mistress blackmail website in England that required him to fill out a form with a lot of personal questions. He wrote:

> I am intensely interested in being blackmailed for a fixed period and a fixed monetary amount but I don't even know if the person I'm dealing with is a woman. Does anyone know about this type of blackmail or this site?

I wrote back:

> Blackmail can be much more fun in fantasy than in reality. In a sense, blackmail is a severe form of psychological bondage. If not practiced carefully with someone you trust, it could have a devastating effect on your future and haunt you the rest of your life. My advice? Build trust with a domme before playing blackmail games.

Then I told the story of Princess William who wanted to give me the names of his business partners, their emails and information about his corporations. He explained how I could ruin him with the information. To get started, I set up a meeting at a hotel. Princess brought sushi for my lunch as commanded. Then he put on a glimmering teddy, wrist and ankle cuffs and a chastity device that prevented an erection. After tying him up, I forced him to sit in a little closet while I ate my lunch. Then I had Princess stand in front of the panoramic window of our twentieth floor suite, exposed to the whole city.

I showed Princess the two keys to his chastity device and explained that unless he started giving me information about his businesses, one of the keys would be flushed down the toilet and the other thrown out the twenty-story window. He begged me not to throw away the keys but could see I was serious about teaching him the real consequences of his blackmail fantasy. He began giving me the names, phone numbers and email addresses of his associates. Then we had a little photo shoot of Princess in his teddy.

A month later I telephoned Princess out of the blue and said he would star in photos on his own website unless he immediately wired funds into my bank account. The amount I required was four times higher than Princess expected. He panicked because he didn't have the cash available and had to do some quick transactions. That was how Princess William learned fantasy was sometimes better than reality. He also knew that any time I wished, I could pull out those pictures and ask for more money. All done with his consent.

> Pigtails served as my sissy maid for a little over a year. A big, burly truck driver, he hauled cattle. I gave him his moniker after the first time I put his long hair in pigtails.

Not all of my clients were wealthy like Princess. Some could not afford to see me regularly, so I chose the most earnest for reduced or no fees at all, depending on what they could offer to my life and my little enterprise. Early after I established my practice, I met a masochist with an intense foot fetish. In his late twenties, six-four and nearly four hundred pounds, he was built like an offensive lineman. Two or three times a month he booked appointments at two-hundred seventy five dollars each, more than he could afford. I did not want to cause his life to derail financially, so I offered him a lifestyle position to give me foot care. He described his service on my online forum.

> I am proud to say I am her personal foot bitch. It is my job to make sure Miss Ann's feet are well taken care of. Miss Ann's feet must be silky smooth and soft at all times. I always become very excited when i serve Miss Ann's feet and last Friday evening was no exception. As always I fill the spa with warm water. This night, as I filled the spa, thoughts of Miss Ann's feet raced through my mind. They are long and lovely. The toes are a perfect size and always painted to perfection. . . . After both feet were scrubbed Miss Ann soaks again. Next I dry Miss Ann's feet and rub them with lotion. This is my favorite part. I find the kinks in the bottom and work them out slowly. "Oh foot bitch that is good," Miss Ann says with Her lower lip pouting and a sexy look on Her face. I just want to suck Her toes so bad but I concentrate at the task at hand. That evening I had the privilege of taking photos of the foot session. I am a very lucky boy. The photos are breathtaking but nothing compared to the real thing.

Not everything was peppermint oil and roses and footbytch's neediness would get on my last nerve. He was jealous of other boys I was seeing, a major no-no for a sub. The submissive's role was duty and selflessness. Footbytch complained that I spent too much time with other subs and didn't pay him enough attention. His self-pity displeased me.

One day footbytch called. "I was thinking it was time to take care of your feet again, Miss. Can I come over on Thursday?"

When he showed up, his poor attitude made me angry. "You aren't fit for this house!" I said.

He stared at me through the glass and sulked on the front porch, pleading with me to let him in. I told him he couldn't come back for three days, no matter how much he begged. I had to teach him his place. After a couple of hours, he went home.

Another time, his self-centered envy landed him in my jail cell. I shared footbytch's saga with my online group.

I thought some of you might benefit from understanding footbytch's recent trip to my "reformatory." I discovered that he was feeling like second fiddle to some of my other subs. You see, for a long time, footbytch was the only boy who served here on a lifestyle basis. He was the first to be plucked from a professional session for more personal service to me. I learned he felt as if he was no longer very important to me, as I am also training other subs to do his normal tasks. It didn't occur to him that because of the vast number of projects I need to accomplish this year, I am building a good-sized stable of subs.

I told footbytch to report to the cage, strip naked, and wait for me there. After a few minutes I went down to find him sitting cross-legged with his head hung low. I locked him in the chains and told him to get on all fours. Without ceremony or even warm up, I started to strike his ass hard with my crop. I did this many times as I told him that his service was indeed important to me and that I need a veritable army of boys to accomplish my goals this year and that he is important.

I then put his face into my feet (the same feet he kisses and cares for) and began to whack him with the big black paddle he normally loves. This time, however, he safeworded very quickly. I realized his pain tolerance is much lower when he knows I'm not happy with him. Normally, I don't punish footbytch with pain because he likes it.

After his paddling I brought my chair into his cell and talked to him in depth about my plans for the year and just how much he is needed in my life. I also explained how his service benefits all of the subs out there who are new and exploring the lifestyle, as he is a great example of a submissive who gives true service.

It is normal for subs to need reassurance from their dommes from time to time. It is also normal for subs to go through periods when they don't feel appreciated enough. I hear it often. A good domina will take the time to get to the bottom of the real problem a submissive has and address it. Sometimes we dommes get so busy, we don't express how deeply we care and just how valued our closest submissives are. I think, like any relationship, we can sometimes take people for granted. The beauty of a D/s relationship is that we have rituals to reinforce the meaning we give to one another's lives. I think footbytch has no doubt just how important he is to my life and to the future of Dungeon Arts.

At one point footbytch decided he needed more gainful employment so I helped him write a resume and coached him through the interview process. His income increased thirty percent overnight after he landed the job. That didn't hurt my world one bit because footbytch loved lavishing presents on me. In a letter to my online group, he publicly acknowledged how he had improved under my tutelage. As a total surprise one day, footbytch handed me thirteenth row seats to see Coldplay at the Murat Theatre, located in a beautiful old Shrine temple. I was thrilled. The concert was one of the best shows I had ever seen.

Another sub, Pigtails, served as my sissy maid for a little over a year. A big, burly truck driver, he hauled cattle. I gave him his moniker after the first time I put his long hair in pigtails. For a sub who craved feminization, how could I resist? Pigtails was sweet and polite and I appreciated his kind words. He wrote:

> I am always excited to serve Miss Ann. When She opens the door and I see Her beautiful smile it truly makes my soul shine. One morning I put on my maid uniform as I always do and spent all day doing house chores that consisted of mopping the kitchen, vacuuming, dusting, doing dishes and laundry. I then prepared and served

dinner, during that time I was told I would be punished later for placing the napkins the wrong way, something She has told me about at least three times.

Pigtail's kink was feminization and extreme humiliation, difficult for most people to comprehend. Deeply submissive people enjoyed humiliation because it made them feel even lower–and that was the goal. Pigtails tried to explain in this post.

> Why would anyone want to be humiliated? I`ve asked myself that question many times. I don't have a complete answer but for me I suspect it has a lot to do with being dominated and controlled.

> About a month ago Maitresse was trying to make a point and told me to do something that I truly did not want to do. When I told Her I would not do it I saw a part of Her I had never seen before. The soft spoken Femme Domme that i had come to know was gone, with a very authoritative voice She demanded that I do it. At that moment I felt completely dominated and controlled, it was a rush that flooded me. That's when I knew how deep my need to be controlled was, it is as deep as my need to serve!

> After reflecting back on that incident many times I realized a big part of my desire was to be humiliated, the domination and control, being forced to do something I would rather not do. I feel that there is more to it than this but I have not found that answer yet.

> I have been into D/s for many years and have experienced what I would consider to be some fairly extreme humiliation. I have been taken to a women's clothing store and forced to try on lingerie and then purchase it, I have

been sent out to sweep the sidewalk wearing a collar and frilly apron.

Since I have been serving Maitresse, She has taken me to a tanning bed wearing stockings and open toed high heels and forced me to start on my sissy tan, tanning while wearing a bra. which I am still required to do, although I have neglected it lately I will be starting to work on it again this week. She has also forced me to answer the door wearing a pink maid's uniform with my hair in pink bows and pigtails for the pizza delivery guy. Please know that at anytime, in any situation I could safeword and everything would stop. I know this but I think that my need to please and be controlled would make it nearly impossible to do so.

Pigtails even became part of my holiday decorations one year. It was safe and, of course, consensual.

I have been involved in BDSM for nearly 20 yrs. In that time I have been in countless scenes and believe me I know the difference between what is safe and what is not. A few days before New Years Eve Maitresse asked me if I would like to serve as a mummified Christmas tree at her New Years Eve party. She explained in detail what she had in mind and that She would make arrangements with a Domme that would NOT be drinking to watch over me. At no time while I was mummified was I in any danger. Even with my appointed Maitresse keeping a close eye on me, Miss Ann was constantly checking on me to make sure I was alright. Both Dommes gave me food and liquids while I was in bondage. . . . I can tell all of you from experience that Miss Ann is very safety minded. If she wasn't I would not serve her. Anyone that has sessioned with Her knows this is true.

Like any job, being a domme sometimes felt repetitive because there was only so much I could do to subs that was new and exciting. Less than a year into doing sessions, work as a professional dominatrix teetered on the edge of being boring. From my perspective I was doing the same routines over and over even though for the subs, everything was still a thrill. Kneeler was run through my standard gauntlet and felt he had an enlightening experience. Afterward he wrote to the online forum.

Miss Ann conducted a thorough telephone interview prior to my first session. She asked many insightful questions. Some of the questions made me slightly uncomfortable as they forced me to think of things in a way that I am unaccustomed to. I was extremely nervous during the interview because Miss Ann seemed to be getting into my head. It was like this was the first time I felt like I could be open, honest–be understood and not ridiculed. After that hour on the phone I was still not sure what to expect but felt like it would be different than anything that I have ever experienced.

After disrobing and hanging up my clothes I assumed a subservient position on the rug while awaiting her return. She returned and made me kiss her shoes while she smacked me with the biggest riding crop that I have ever seen for my perceived lack of enthusiasm. That thing is really painful!!! Miss Ann made me kiss the collar before she put it on me while explaining that once it was on I would be doing what she wanted me to do and that I would have no control. After the collar was on she attached the leash and I became aroused by her taking control of me. I was made to back up to a post while Miss

Ann measured my manhood and then ridiculed its size. Then I was mummified to the post and I thought this was really not bad at all. After she was done I began to worry when she put a hood over my head and then cut holes to expose my nipples and my cock. Still I thought this was kind of cool. Then one of my nipples became red hot, and then the other. I could not see what she was doing to me. I could only feel the pain.

Hello Kneeler,

Thank you for writing about your experience in my dungeon. I already know you are going to be a good submissive by how well you follow my instructions. In reading your account I realize your brain was working overtime when your sight was deprived in that hood. The hotness on your nipples was magnified by your mind. I was dripping very soft safety wax on your nipples and allowing it to drip on the tender part of my wrist at the same time, to make sure the drips were not too hot. The biggest crop you have ever seen is actually the smallest crop that the Stockroom sells! The mind is so powerful.

I must say I LOVE it when a submissive is trembling and under my control. I was pleased by how far you went with me. And that you pushed yourself for me. I am most pleased that you trusted me to take you there.

A submissive contacted me from London and arranged to come over for a week-long stay. He said he had served at the Other World Kingdom (OWK) in the Czech Republic so I thought he was experienced and ready to handle scening with me. The OWK was a commercial femdom or female dominant facility located in the buildings and grounds of a sixteenth century chateau. OWK considered itself a separate state, a matriarchy, and had its own "passports" and currency. The sub from London, however, was not what he represented himself to be. He violated his contract terms within hours of arriving. He also brought a parcel of illegal drugs which I flushed down the toilet. That pissed him off.

I had brought in another domme from out of town, Lady Evelyn, to help out. The sub was told he would be locked in my cell behind its steel door if he violated the rules he had agreed upfront to follow. His contract gave me no choice but to inflict punishment when he disobeyed. His behavior was bizarre and afterward he wrote an uncommonly creative account of his visit, not entirely based on fact. It is fair to say it came partly from his fantasy of what might read as good D/s fiction.

> I am an English submissive slave. I was intrigued by the work of Miss Ann. I decided to apply for slave training at Miss Ann's home. I figure myself a hard core slave. I have spent time at the other world kingdom and regularly serve dominant ladies in Europe. I was due to serve at Miss Ann's home for a period of one week. The dates were between October 28th to Nov 4th.
>
> I arrived at Indianapolis airport very tired and jet legged. Awaiting my luggage at baggage, I spotted the very beautiful Miss Ann immediate. My luggage had been lost by Delta Airlines, but was delivered to her home later.
>
> My first impressions was she was tall and very good looking. Miss Ann took me to a German bar in Indianapolis first off, for a light lunch and refreshment. We then headed

off to collect Lady Evelyn, and by the time we reached back at Miss Ann's home I was dog tired.

The first night she allowed me to sleep peacefully in the dungeon on the sofa bed. The next morning it was time to sign my contract, prepared by Miss Ann. I read it carefully. It appeared to cover everything from personal hygiene to smoking breaks for good behavior. Soon as the contract had been signed by both mistress and slave. things began to change dramatically. My shoes were removed, as it appeared shoes were forbidden amongst slaves in Miss Ann's home,

This did make me feel very humble, as it removes your male aggression and makes you feel humble, Next I was made to fit the CB2000. [male chastity device] Miss Ann kept the key around her neck. The day was short as I was allowed to sleep in because of my jet lag.

I remember my first lunch, the table was laid for two in the dining room, Lady Evelyn and Miss Ann took their places on the comfortable chairs. To my horror and humiliation I was to sit at Miss Anns very beautiful stocking feet. Throughout the dining, Miss Ann would feed me scraps from her plate, and I was made to beg like a dog for the scraps, much to the Ladies amusement.

I was then ordered to give Miss Ann's feet some beauty treatment, I had brought from England a complete foot care kit from the body shop. It was now soon time for bed. This time Lady Evelyn chained one ankle to a floor chain for my nights sleep. I was left a mobile phone to call Miss Ann at 10am the next morning to come release me. I was awoken by angry feet steps coming down the dungeon stairs. It was Miss Ann. I had never seen her so furious,

I had overslept, and to my horror my CB2000 had come off in the night. It was not tampered with or neither did i masturbate, but Miss Ann was not convinced, to CB2000 wearers you will know that if the spacer is not fitted it is possible to drop off, and I also had the points of intrigue fitted.

I was too late, I was to be punished, This was my first time in the steel cage, I was stripped naked and chained like an animal within the bars. I will admit i was feeling cheated, as I was honest about over sleeping and the CB2000 escape was an accident. After a couple of hours in the dark cell I was given breakfast, for some reason i had sulked, this. I will warn fellow subs who are thinking of a stay at Miss Ann's, will not mellow her but enrage her. It just got me more and more time in the cage. I had refused to eat, and a bucket was then provided to wash. This I refused too. I had fire in me and I was not complying at all.

Eventually after sulking I was given one more chance, I was let out and once more forced to eat the cold cereal. This freaked Miss Ann, I demanded I had enough and wanted to fly out. Miss Ann agreed to this then left the room. I sat in the dungeon feeling awful, and decided to crawl up the stairs and grovel to Miss Ann. I crawled through the house to Miss Ann's office and I knelt humbly while she was on the phone. When Miss Ann was finished, I offered my apology.

I must have been an awful slave, I will admit this. Miss Ann reluctantly agreed to let me stay, and told me to go to the dungeon and wait on my knees. Eventually Miss Ann, accompanied by Lady Evelyn, came to the Dungeon. Miss Ann had decided that if I stayed I must serve 12 hours solid in the cage. I was given a book to read on Thomas

Jefferson and i was to be tested on my knowledge. The steel cage is an awful place. It is dark and you lose sense of time. It is solitary confinement and once the door shuts you are alone. The boiler noise cuts in all the time. I was lucky as one of Miss Ann's cats was left in there with me, but once the cat went through a hole, I was alone.

My neck was chained to a ring concreted in to the floor by a small chain, and my ankle chained too. Above me in the house I could hear clicking of the Ladies shoes and got excited when I thought the noises were coming to me, but they never did. Eventually Lady Evelyn came to me. The door opened, and the light squinted my eyes. It was a great relief that I was to be given my first cigarette. These were rationed to me every three hours, when you are bored. A cigarette is a welcome relief.

Lady Evelyn handed me the cigarette and lighter to keep. She advised to smoke a little at a time. It was awful knowing I had 400 in my case. Hours seemed to go by, i was bored senseless. Lady Evelyn came occasionally to check on my water. It was then I begged her to let me out, but my begging was to come to nothing, By now I was getting uncomfortable and restless.

Miss Ann herself came down to me. A chair was brought in for her to sit comfortably. She looked stunning in pretty shoes and lovely dress. She just sat and blew smoke in my eyes, Her shoe dangled before me, but I could not reach to kiss her foot, as my chain was too short. I started to beg and plead to be let out. I wanted to serve, but she left me in darkness once more. I could have sworn I had safe worded,or I believed in my mind I had. I was now thinking I was going to be in the cage for a week, and began to plot my escape.

PART II

As I explained in part one. I had come to serve Miss Ann and Lady Evelyn for a full week of servitude from England, not knowing just how severe the cage is. Miss Ann I believed was to be the last time I was to see her that day. The last visit I had I believed was late night,but it could had been four in the afternoon. I had lost track of time. I did all kinds of pros and cons in my mind as to if I should attempt to break out. I had no idea how long I was to remain chained up in this dark hole. All I knew was that I wanted to serve, but I hated being here in the cage. I had indeed estimated that I had now been so disobedient that the four days I had left before returning to England was going to spent here in the small cage. My mind was a swim with what to do. I knew Miss Ann was now not to be underestimated and I believed that it was Her intention to keep me there until the day i was to leave. Also in my mind, I knew I had friends vacating in warm Miami. I had decided enough was enough, I had tried groveling pleading for release, but it never came.

I began by straining my neck with hard yanks and tugging at the collar. It was not easy but eventually the rivets broke freeing me from the collar. My first thoughts was that Miss Ann, If she finds me now, she will be pretty mad at me. So I decided to go for the break out. Next was the cuff to my ankle. By doing the same with my collar the chain busted, freeing my leg. It was great to stand and stretch out. Next was the door. First I was punching it with my fist, but the noise was very loud. I could not believe no one had heard the noise. I had thoughts that they had both gone out. The punching was proving useless, so I sat down and thought for a while what to do next. I started to get angry, because I couldn't get out, Whatever way I was in deep trouble now. I couldnt fix my bonds back on, and I was at the point of no return. I then kicked at the door with my bare feet, just kicking and kicking, half expecting Miss Ann to come down to stop the noise. Then with one final kick, the door fell to the ground. I was shaking and shivering, but also scared. I was a little scared as i clambered from my prison. The first thing I grabbed was a cigarette, I was very very nervous, I knew it was wrong for me to be free. I dared not venture up in to the house. I quickly got dressed and just sat and smoked. I could see by the sky light, at the top of the dungeon steps, that it was daylight. This pleased me because I did not want it to be the middle of the night.

Soon I began to hear noises above, someone was up. My heart was racing to what Miss Ann would make of it all. Foot steps descended the Dungeon steps, it was Miss Ann. Her first reaction was of shock. I said immediately that I want to go home, I have had enough. She inspected the damage, but did not get angry with me. I offered to fix the damaged door, but Miss Ann said she was going to replace it with an iron door. Miss Ann said to make myself comfortable. I could live like a human, I was no longer her slave. Miss Ann dropped me to the airport. I went down to Florida, found my friends, and tried to enjoy myself, but deep down I was very very unhappy with myself. I have always wanted to be a slave to a Lady and here I was free, but unhappy. I kept going to internet cafes, begging forgiveness. Me and Miss Ann remain on very good terms. I have offered to return again to complete my sentence in her steel cage.

ChapterEight

Lady Liza apprenticed with me and was running sessions on her own in no time. Part of her responsibility was to maintain the dungeon. Atmosphere was everything and a lot of behind the scenes work went into preparing for clients. She cleaned the furniture, replaced the candles in the wrought iron sconces and removed dripped wax. Liza never cared for her chores but dutifully complied.

She was professional in session but her life was a disaster in the real world. She lived with a guy she called her boyfriend who was a slacker with precarious employment so she had to juggle the slacker, the DJ from the strip bar where she performed and other liaisons, including her Master Scott. At one point she was even a lesbian. Her identity crisis was exhausting. However, she was the belle of the ball at my house. Effective in session and strict about the rules, she gave enough for me to endure her arrogance.

One March afternoon I sat in my office, staring out the window. A sub had called a couple days before, seeking the services of Dungeon Arts for the first time. He was running a bit late. I opened the door to an unkempt man in his late fifties. The energy he emitted mirrored his bedraggled looks. Seemed like the perfect session for Liza. I went through the whole madame spiel and locked up his cash while Liza lingered in the background then took him downstairs. Thirty minutes later I heard her heels on the stairs.

"Miss Ann, the sub says he wants to jerk off in the dungeon," Liza said, poker-faced.

"That's not happening! Go back and ask him what's more important, serving you or his precious orgasm."

Liza walked down the stairs but was back in my office after a few minutes.

"He chose his orgasm, Miss Ann."

"Have him report to me immediately!"

He made his way up from the dungeon as I waited hands on hips by the front door.

"So your precious little orgasm was more important than serving Lady Liza and me?"

With his head dropped low he mumbled, "Sorry, Miss."

"Yes, you're sorry! You're nothing more than a worm to me. Now get out of my house and don't ever come back!"

The moment he was on the porch, I stomped my foot as if shooing away an stray animal. "Scat!"

A sub named funtoy, who was to become one of my favorites, posted this letter after our first session.

This is a letter to talk about the beginning of my journey with Miss Ann and our first session together.

Needless to say I was very nervous when I first arrived, but she made me feel very comfortable after a small chat. From my point of view this helped tremendously to settle myself and feel more at ease in her company. I was not nervous in a scared way but more like not knowing what she might have planned for me on that first day. She calls me a blank slate since I have no particular fetishes which turned out to be a good thing, since I am open to many things not beyond my hard limits.

After our short conversation I felt truly at ease in her honorable presence and then she instructed me to follow her to her dungeon. Upon entrance to the dungeon I was instructed to light all of the candles along the walls of the dark space. After this task was completed I was ordered to kneel and given the honor of kissing her feet, which was a wonderful feeling I might add.

When she was satisfied with that task being completed I was instructed to take my clothes off and be in a kneeling position awaiting her return from upstairs. While kneeling there waiting for her, to return I found myself to be in an excited and slightly nervous state once again, since I had no idea of Her plans for me. When she returned, I began my learning process and training. . . . learning how she likes my chin up looking at her while I am kneeling. . . . learning how if I did not do tasks as instructed I would feel the hard sting of her crop. I realized at this moment that the training I was receiving from Her has been what I had craved for a long time.

I gazed in amazement at her as she prepared the tools she would be using on me this day. She brought out these very long latex strips from the other room which I helped her untangle. At this time I must admit my nervousness in helping her prepare these latex strips, having no idea what she had in mind to do with them. After untangling all of the latex I watched her grab this long rataan pole which she carefully wrapped in a towel. She instructed me to stand next to a pole with my back straight and chin up. She placed the pole over my shoulders and behind my neck and instructed me to place my arms outward with my wrists over the ends of the pole.

Then she proceeded to wrap my arm in the latex and then around the pole, my head and my stomach proceeding to my other arm. I then realized I was in her complete control, helpless to move anywhere. The only thing that kept running through my mind at that time was my deep and sincere wish to please her. She then told me that I was the first sub that she had ever tried this particular scene with and I felt a great sense of honor in knowing I was the first one.

Miss Ann at this time wished to take some pictures but there was a delay in the camera being ready. At this point my arms were starting to fall asleep but I did not say anything. But soon I could not feel my fingers and mentioned this to her.

I so dearly wanted to continue so I could please her by posing this way but she would hear nothing of it and immediately removed the latex wraps and releasing my arms so they could hang to my side and regain feeling. I felt ashamed as if I had failed her but she was very understanding and caring at this moment making sure I was alright first before W/we would try the pose again. At that moment I felt truly cared for by Miss Ann which was something I did not honestly expect when I first arrived that day.

Everyone reading this must understand that I had never been in the hands of a professional Domme before so I truly did not know what to expect. After she was kind enough to let my hands regain their feeling she wrapped me in the latex again and placed candles in my hands. She then took photos of me as her new subbie candelabra (smiles).

After I completed that task for her I was given the great honor of massaging her feet for a long time. I remember feeling thankful for this honor because I could visually tell that my massage was giving her pleasure. I was even able to sneek a couple kisses onto her feet during this time which she also seemed to enjoy.

When she was finished with me massaging her feet, I was instructed to clean all of the latex and other things that were used on me while she left the dungeon. After cleaning up I was ordered to meet her in her office.

She and I chatted about our session for a while before I was given the honor once again of kissing her feet before my departure. I can honestly say that the time I spent with the beautiful Miss Ann that day was one of the most memorable and cherished times of my life. I am grateful and honored to have had the opportunity of having her time and training. For any subs interested in having a session with Miss Ann I would highly recommend it. I promise it will be a safe, honorable and unforgettable experience which you will never forget.

Here is another letter from Funtoy about a later session.

I entered the door and was immediately instructed to kneel before her and kiss her beautiful feet that were adorned in wonderful shiny, black, spiked heels. I truly am honored with this ritual as it puts me in my place, as her submissive, immediately as I enter the door. As always Miss Ann looked immaculate. She was dressed in a black, long coat and short skirt with black nylons and garters. After telling me I could rise she instructed me to follow her to her office as she finished some work on the computer. Kneeling next to Her i watched her work and realized how busy she is at all times with this group and all of her other activities. This truly made me realize how lucky I am to be in her presence even if for a short amount of time.

After finishing her work she ordered me to follow her down to the dungeon. As soon as we were there I was again ordered to kneel and kiss her feet and then instructed to strip naked and be in a kneeling position for her when she returned in a few minutes. At this time, like my first session with her, my mind was racing in anticipation and wonder as to what her pleasure would be with me. When she returned I kissed her feet once again and She made sure I was aware who was in charge as she slapped my bare bottom a couple of times with Her crop.

She then told me that we would be working to perfect my being her candelabra. Something that we had started on in my first session. She had given much thought as to how to do this without my arms falling asleep as they had done in our first session. Her new ideas worked much better as she wrapped me in the latex strips carefully using my whole body as her canvas. I was smiling inside hearing her comments of pleasure of how I looked even better this time. Since I was completely wrapped I had no use of my arms, my torso was held tight to a pole, and my eyes were covered. I could hear her move what I thought was furniture around on the floor. Not knowing what she was doing is always a rush of excitement and apprehension all at the same time.

When she finished taking photos of me as her little candelabra boy I heard her move one more piece of furniture. Though I didn't know it at the time it turned out to be a chair she placed directly in front of me. At this time I could feel the tip of her crop first caressing and then tapping my cock. The sensations were increasing as she tapped and then began to slap the head of my cock with her crop.

First there was pleasure in the taps and then the pain of the slaps. Sensations of pain and pleasure were criss crossing my body and mind. She told me I must be enjoying it since my cock was growing and that a man's cock never lies. I could hear her laugh with delight as she slapped my cock hard and my body would writhe in pain. My only thoughts at this time were to hang on and honor her with as much enjoyment as possible because I so dearly want to please her. This pleasure for her did continue for some time.

And then, unfortunately, my one arm fell asleep and I told Miss Ann about this as I had been instructed to from the beginning of the session. Even though this ended her pleasure with me I was grateful for her caring of me by letting my arms down to regain their feeling. I trust Miss Ann completely in the knowledge, and now experience, that she will not permanently harm me. For me this is a huge step since I do not trust anyone very easily. I feel very grateful, honored and lucky to have such a beautiful and trustworthy Maitresse live so close to me. And I dearly hope I give Her the pleasure she desires as one of her submissives.

Thank You Miss Ann for being such an incredible, trustworthy and beautiful Maitresse.

I wrote to my online group about funtoy's trust in me and how it enabled him to walk through one of his biggest fears. He dreaded being feminized.

Today funtoy came to visit me again. I decided to begin testing the trust he says he places in me and do something a little different than our previous sessions.

Funtoy was told to dress in an open bottomed girdle with garters and white thigh high stockings and wait for me in the normal bowed position. When I returned to the dungeon to find him waiting, he was trembling a bit, just below the surface. I immediately started to feed from that.

I had him present his hands to me and I slowly wrapped them loosely in rope. When his hands were wrapped I secured them above his head in an eyebolt in the dungeon ceiling. His hands were tied and secured in such a way that the more he struggled the tighter his binding became.

I tied his feet together the same way and placed a hood on his head. When a submissive is tied, vulnerable and deprived of sight the sensations he feels are intensified. Funtoy is normally pretty sensitive, I thought adding this level of vulnerability would make him quiver. I was right.

At first I began swatting him mildly with my crop. I knew he was craving my touch, so I began to very lightly touch him. I touched his nipple first, very very lightly. He was drinking me in. I love how a simple touch from me can make him quiver.

I put the clover clamps on his nipples and I thought he'd jump out of his skin. funtoy is far from a pain slut, but he likes to endure for me. He loves pleasing. Then out of nowhere, I struck his cock one time with my crop, not too hard, but hard enough to make a loud smacking noise. He almost jumped out of his skin! His wrist bondage was such that the more he squirmed, the tighter his bonds got. The tighter the bonds, the more helpless he felt. Then the more helpless he felt, the deeper in he went.

I then remembered my nice rabbit fur vampire mitt. First I stroked his chest and back with the nice soft fur–the side without the tiny spikes–it had the soothing effect I wanted. funtoy didn't realize that he was soon to feel the bite of the tiny spikes in the glove. That completely caught him off guard.

I was impressed by how he walked into his fear with me. How, even though he was bound and helpless, he ultimately knew his trust was in me, his Domme, and that I would walk him right through his fear and ultimately take care of him. He trusted me even though he was tied, and helpless in a dungeon full of all kinds of painful toys.

This may seem like a rather mild session for some of you, however, funtoy is still a novice. Sometimes small things in a scene seem very big when you are tied and blindfolded. It's fun to get big reactions from submissives even with the smallest acts. I only used rope, a vampire mitt, and a crop for this session . . . not much in terms of toys. The real journey is in the mind.

For me, the point of D/s is the power exchange and the building of trust between me and my subs, step by step.

The following letter was written to my online forum about the issue of trust.

My post today is about an aspect of behavior, on the submissive's part in a D/s relationship, that Miss Ann has asked for me to write about to the group.

I spent time with Miss Ann, and a lifestyle Domme friend of hers, last night and had a wonderful discussion about many, many topics. One of the topics that arose during that discussion was something I had been thinking about since I first met Miss Ann many months ago. At that time Miss Ann and I had already had our phone interview and then I had completed my first face to face interview with Her. After telling her of my hard limits in the interviews I felt there was nothing more to say about what I WANTED to happen in our sessions.

When I looked around her wonderfully equipped dungeon I saw many things that intrigued me and that I aspired to try at some point, but not once have I ever asked Miss Ann to try those things on me. As a submissive I never thought it was my place to ASK for anything from her. When I schedule a session with her I do not even request a time of the day for the session to happen. I leave the time of the session up to her as i feel i should be there when she wants me to be there.

My point in all of this for you submissives out there is to find a Domme that you trust and care for and when you do find her, and when in a session with her, leave your wants at the door. I will give you an example as to why I say this and how rewarding it can be when you leave those wants unspoken.

Recently, I visited Miss Ann after she had invited me to a big yard sale she was having in conjunction with a neighborhood festival that was happening in her area. I looked around at all she was selling that day and even bought a few things. After making my purchases I asked her if she would show me all of the recent improvements She had made in her home since the last time I was there. She readily agreed to show me around and I was amazed at the transformation she had accomplished in the whole first story of her home.

But one thing that really struck me was a new piece of equipment she had recently acquired from one of her loyal submissives. This piece of equipment, that she calls a Fantasy Rack, was huddled in the corner of her sunroom as it was too large to fit down in her dungeon. I was completely amazed by this piece of equipment when I viewed it and I knew in my mind that being strapped to it was something that i would dearly like to try. However, at no time during that visit did I indicate to Miss Ann my interest in that "Fantasy Rack." I did not think it would be proper to hint around about my interest in it, nor even speak about it in glowing terms. I simply left her home that day hoping that someday She would honor me by putting me into it.

Two weeks later I scheduled another appointment with Miss Ann and told her what day I was available and she set the time for the session. As usual I had no idea what she would do to me that day. After spending quite a bit of time in her dungeon during that session she told me that she had a surprise for me and brought me upstairs. It was then that she informed me that she would be putting me into the "fantasy rack" and that I would be the first submissive that she had put into that piece of equipment. In my mind I was ecstatic as it was a great honor to be the first submissive she had used in that piece of equipment and I had a magical feeling that day while in her home.

That feeling came from the fact that SHE WANTED to put me in that rack without me disclosing to Her my desires to be put into it. I had trusted in Miss Ann that someday she would want to have me in that rack and the fact I had never said anything to her made me feel like I had truly pleased her by being used in that fashion. In other words it meant much more to her that she had put me there than it did to me that I wanted to be strapped into it. For me this was the ultimate feeling of pleasing the Domme and also a deeper sense of worth to her for having not asked for it. I know it would not have felt nearly as fulfilling, for her or me, had I asked her to do this to me. My point in all of this is to find a Domme that you trust and then trust in her to do what she wants. In my small opinion if you do that then you will have a much greater feeling of being truly submissive.

Having said all of this I want to make it clear that I am NOT telling the subs out there not to be open and talk with their Dommes. Open lines of communication should flow both ways in a true D/s relationship and is a very important aspect of that relationship. But in my opinion a sub should never discuss his wants in a session DURING a session. There are times when a sub can discuss his desires or needs during a casual conversation and then once said then leave it alone. It has been my experience that the Domme will detect, learn and know what the submissive likes and wants. It is my belief that a sub need not repeat himself many times to try and accomplish that. To me, a submissive is there for what the Domme wants and should not grovel for what he wants. In the example I gave above I found myself much happier inside being surprised by Miss Ann in that she wanted to do to me what I had only fantasized about in my mind. When I discussed this with Miss Ann she seemed to be so pleased with me in that I "got it" and that I understood what it truly means to be submissive. My hope is that this open letter will help the subs out there in realizing that a true D/s relationship is about pleasing the Domme and not being pleasured yourself. My belief is that if the sub approaches the relationship in this manner then he will be surprised at how fulfilling it can be to be submissive.

Before long Lady Liza started taking sessions and hanging out at a dungeon in a nearby town. The Fluttering Menace rented out a tiny bungalow that had been converted into a full-on house of domination where Liza started getting into some dark stuff. She consented to being a full-time professional submissive and allowed men she didn't know to tie her up and spank her in scenes with the Menace. I knew the Menace was an experienced domme who wouldn't have allowed Liza to be harmed.

At barely five-feet tall the Menace managed to be commanding in long dreadlocks, false eyelashes and extreme make-up, including rhinestones meticulously applied as eyeliner. She was a goth who fashioned herself as a peculiar geisha in witchy gowns, corsets and shawls. A downtown martini bar was the venue for her informal monthly gathering of mistresses. I loved dressing up and going out to sip on cosmos as I talked the night away with other dommes. My conventional looks made me feel like Marilyn Munster, the wholesome blond cousin living among freaks. Subs always showed up and, of course, we graced them with the honor of buying us drinks. The Menace sounded insightful when she talked about domming and the camaraderie with other dominant women helped open up my world and inspire me.

> Being called a prostitute unnerved me almost more than anything. I wasn't getting paid to have sex, but a lot of people didn't understand that.

An old friend called one day and invited me to a party in the neighborhood. This made me anxious because I hadn't seen some of these people since starting my business. When I went into D/s, I simply wanted to do something different to engage my brain. From old friends I hoped to hear, "Mely, good to see you!" Instead, they said, "Look! It's the dominatrix!" I became a character to them and living out-of-the-box meant standing alone. Earlier a friend even commented, "It's a shame you have to make your living in the sex industry." Being called a prostitute unnerved me almost more than anything. I wasn't getting paid to have sex, but a lot of people didn't understand that. Come party night, I was relieved the crowd turned out to be friendly people who were comfortable with my choices. I was questioned but not entirely ridiculed. Sure, some people poked fun at me but I tried not to internalize it.

Nothing stirred in my house for a couple of days after the party. D/s lifestyle scening had been phased out of my personal life. Somewhere along the way, the carefree days with roommates had also faded away. Mistress Claudia had moved out and the latex kitten found his dream girl and left, leaving Antonio and me alone. Antonio had a stabilizing effect on me as I worked at keeping my little enterprise together. The guys got the therapy they craved while I topped scenes for money and didn't often enter into dommespace. Power exchanges had become clinical and my work was rarely satisfying.

Every night I fell asleep, asking, "Why?" The question embedded itself in my head. What was I doing? Beseeching the universe, I cried, "If you want me to stay in this wacky career, you better give me a mission or I'm quitting."

I decided to try to articulate my mission and sat down at my computer. Why was I in this predicament? One, I was giving these guys a safe place in which to explore their fantasies and bizarre needs. Two, it wasn't healthy for people to keep their true selves repressed. Even so, I didn't see the connections. The big picture wasn't in sight and every draft I typed sounded more pretentious than the last.

Reminiscing about the people I loved, I thought about the old guilt-free days, working for someone else, my endless dinner parties, hitting the galleries and how much fun it was to be a regular at the Chatterbox. Three days working on a mission at my computer ended as an exercise in futility. It seemed time to update my resume and find another sales job. Having an employer define my job was easier than being an entrepreneur and having to clarify my own purpose and the steps necessary to fulfill it.

At the end of the third day's attempt to write a mission, I opened a bottle of wine and went to my dungeon to say goodbye to the D/s world. In not finding a purpose for my career, I felt I had failed. I wanted back the comfort of the corporate life where I'd had success. Besides, I couldn't handle people thinking of me as a hooker anymore. I needed a sign and decided to sit there until something or someone gave me instructions on what to do next.

After a while I heard a single word come from the dark of my dungeon.

"Actualization."

The sound was a plural voice like a choir. Although I didn't fully understand, the word actualization sounded like something I believed in. It fit what I'd been trying to accomplish.

Then a single voice said, "Write it and it will become reality. After all, I authored this country."

Who was that? Thomas Jefferson?

I ran upstairs to look up the word actualization and remembered Maslow's hierarchy of needs from a Psychology 101 class. The need to build self esteem was required for self-actualization. Every closeted sub I had known lacked self-esteem or self-respect. For me, the main element of self-respect was honesty, but submissives were blocked by a fear of judgment of their compulsions and weird fantasies. How could any of them achieve self-respect if they couldn't be open to the truth about their deepest selves?

I gave submissives acceptance and a safe place to express their true selves. With my help they could begin to feel validated. I had always tried to understand and help them. At that point I started to quickly write my mission.

Mission

To advance the actualization of the individual
via the education, exploration, and practice
of realistic and healthy lifestyle D/s.

While The Reformatory is femme domme in
its leadership, it respects and acknowledges individuals
from all roles and orientations.

The work of The Reformatory is to create a
forum free of religious and societal taboo, dedicated to
understanding what is healthy within the
context of D/s.

It then occurred to me that I needed an additional statement which laid out a platform for advancing my new mission–a manifesto.

A Manifesto

Trust
is the foundation upon which D/s can sit
A D/s relationship be it
professional,
friendship,
or love,
is a relationship.

Relationships thrive in an environment of honesty. Honesty means we own the words we give to one other. We are careful to back our words with fact and action.

The dominant is first accountable to the submissive.

She must own the words she gives to herself and to others.
Her words are always substantiated in fact and action.
She must go to where her submissive is as an individual
and meet him there.
Only then can she guide him into his private shadowland.

Only then can she transform him.

I believe for those who have a proclivity to be
dominant or submissive
we must have a platform for expression.
It is healthy to express this part of our psyche.
Conversely, it is unhealthy to leave it unexplored.

If our fear prevents the expression of our hearts,
we are likely not to self-actualize.

A dynamic educational exploration and practice
of healthy D/s
has the best chance for success in a
well-ordered, safe, friendly, trusting,
and confidential environment.
I am taught primarily by submissives
and will continue to follow that path.
Just as a cabinet of subordinates advise our president,
my personal cabinet of submissives give me advice.

Further, my submissives have great influence over
my personal direction and decisions.
The final decision, however, is always mine.

I seek quality, not quantity.
It is said only two percent of the population enters into
self-actualization.
I believe more than that can achieve it.

I GIVE YOU
permission to be liberated from fear.

December 2002

ChapterNine

I didn't want to start a revolution or anything, I was just trying to help the people in my small orbit. Inspired by my calling for the advancement of education to break down social and religious taboos, I decided to reinforce my mission in an academic light. Learning more about the scientific study of human interaction made sense so I enrolled in a sociology class at a local university.

One of the class topics was about the constraints society puts on individuals who break away from the mainstream to explore new territory. It was a lesson on herd behavior. The professor used as an example Jack Nicholson's audacious character in *One Flew Over the Cuckoo's Nest* and the lengths to which the asylum staff went to make him comply with their rules. The professor also discussed the sexual boundaries Madonna pushed and John Lennon's peace crusade. Both of them suffered push-back for their unconventional lifestyles and opinions. It appeared to me that causes were advanced by people stepping outside their comfort zones. In some cases, an individual breaking from the herd was labeled insane.

For me, D/s had morphed from a shocking hobby into a full-on spiritual journey. I was a long way from the chat rooms and not just getting my rocks off anymore. I was literally changing some of these guys' lives. All the signs and omens had led me to this point and everything finally made sense. I had to take their hands and lead them into their own brave, new world. The only way to achieve true happiness was to bask honestly in oneself, a world of unfiltered self-actualization.

And it wasn't just the subs. It was me, too. I was happy. Unbound by conventional work and living, life was good. Sure it was weird, but I was being who I really was. The definition of beauty was always unique to the individual. Every person, no matter what creed, color or kink secretly wants to shine. I was a dominatrix with a mission, shedding a little light into the lives of the closeted.

Over time a more sophisticated crowd started to frequent my Yahoo! group. The forum became a platform for accomplished people who wanted to feed their intellects along with their sexual desires. Everyone was welcomed. I decided to change the name of my Yahoo! group to the Reformatory because it was a place to learn and re-form ideas.

With a revitalized attitude I challenged people in my Yahoo! group to step up their game. The world needed to know about life in D/s. I wasn't hitting the streets, screaming about being kinky and proud, but I passionately advanced my mission to anyone who would pay attention.

Subs in the group began taking their writing contributions more seriously and the content we fed on became heady and robust.

A cross-dresser named Greta lived a secret life and loved the acceptance The Reformatory provided. Hiding her habit from the outside world had taken its toll.

> For the lifestyle cross-dresser, such as myself, the feeling is not merely the act of wearing clothing determined as feminine, but also to emulate a woman in all ways except the biological. Thus we feel the need to change everything from our postures to the very thoughts which spur our actions. We become in touch with our emotions, learn to listen, to communicate as effectively as only a woman can. We do not wish to insult a woman through emulation, or to take anything away from their natural power, and we acknowledge that the pain inherent to the gender is something we shall never experience physically or perhaps even emotionally. . . .
>
> The one binding factor that brings all cross-dressers together is the need to be accepted for what we truly are. For myself, it has been a heartbreaking journey. I suffered two failed marriages because of it and lived with an almost unbearable sense of loneliness and isolation. One of my many wishes has been to find a female soul-mate who can incorporate it into our lives–from the simplest things, like going shopping together, sharing a glass of wine with a good movie as a backdrop and exploring both my need to understand women and her needs as a woman. This is a dream that many of my peers share.
>
> Finding such a partner, especially in Indiana, has been close to impossible. This is a state which still adheres to

gender specifics in their very basic form. Women have to act and dress a certain way, as do men. The indoctrination which happens during the formative years leads to an attitude of fear and loathing for those who cross these lines. What it all boils down to is the need for a safe place where such prejudices do not exist.

I taught that a person was unable to self-actualize without walking into his fear. In this particular case, a man confessed his interest in bondage but didn't have the willpower to tell his wife.

> I'm 32 years old male, married and have one child. I'm a big "clean cut" guy (6'-5" 215 pounds). I live and work on the north side of Indy. I'm shy and reserved. I'm afraid my friends will think I'm weird or strange if they find out about my passion for bondage. I've been into bondage for about 15 years. I have never told anyone about my interest. I feel I'm a submissive, because I like the feeling of being restrained. The only way I can do that is by self bondage. Over the years I've made many restraints to assist me. I've also collected a large amount of handcuffs, leg irons, chains, locks, and collars. I usually pull the stuff out to play with when I get home from work. I'm not into whipping or much pain, or being someone's slave for a long period. I wouldn't mind finding someone with like mind for a discreet occasional visit.

Many submissives were shy and I wanted to address this particular concern so I wrote the following reply.

> Thanks for writing your introduction. I understand as a shy person it is a big step for you to begin to open up

honestly about who you are in terms of your hunger for bondage, evidenced by your large collection of restraints and self-bondage practices. The truth is that many people like you crave bondage and restraint. They are at college, the office, your church, maybe even in your family. Many people are kinky. The problem is they are afraid to talk about it. I find if practiced carefully, bondage can be therapeutic for the submissive. A positive benefit might be a pleasant sensation induced by rendering an individual vulnerable and helpless. A therapeutic benefit is long-lasting and might be achieved through guided meditation or hypnosis while in bondage. A long lasting benefit might even lead to greater self-actualization of the individual.

I accepted married clients to give them safe space but always felt uncomfortable if they were deceiving their spouses. In some ways our professional relationship was more authentic than the one they had waiting at home. The majority of men posting in my group were seeking advice on real-life crises because their relationships were dishonest. I wrote to my group with an example about a disturbed cross-dresser.

I was thinking this morning about the selfishness of married men who cheat on their spouses. Thinking about how they try to use women like myself to satisfy their kink. I thought about all the submissives I've known who top from the bottom and try to pass it off as service. "Relationships thrive in an environment of honesty. Honesty means we own the words we give to one other. We are careful to back our words with fact and action."

(My Manifesto)

Last week I was contacted again by a cross-dresser who saw me once in session about a year ago. He is terribly conflicted. You see, he is in a long term relationship with his vanilla girlfriend. He gives her his firsts. She gets the presents and European vacations. She has no interest in his kinky desire to play with strap-ons, for instance. She thinks all that play is wrong and immoral and deviant. Yet, he wants this play and he wants an emotionally connected relationship on the side with a female dominant.

In reality his girlfriend doesn't accept him for who he is as an individual. And he doesn't accept her as the vanilla individual she is. He's looking to cheat. She's closed-minded and planning to stay that way. He's kinky and can't help but want to explore it. She doesn't care about his deepest desires. And he doesn't care about being faithful to her.

I want for everyone to live fully according to who they are. The lesson here is not to worry so much about what others think. What is important is that we are living true to who we are inside and face our personal fears. Even if it means dissolving relationships that are not in harmony with who we are. If the person truly loves us, they will accept us. And if they don't accept us as we are, do we want them anyway? That's called unconditional love.

My submissive Niles, whom I renamed "funtoy," was a sponge. He was sincere about wanting to explore but didn't know where to start. He was what I called a pure sub, into the mental aspects of meaningful service more than the corporeal. Our sessions often included challenging physical scenarios such as bondage, but the overriding theme of our work was always psychological. I admired Niles' earnest efforts at self-discovery. He made sure he presented himself as a blank slate each session and claimed his path to self-actualization started in my dungeon during his first visit.

I was getting the intellectual stimulation I needed and no longer looked at these guys as a means to my end, but I became a means to theirs. I encouraged subs to write about their experiences. Niles honored me when he wrote the following years after we first met.

> I delved into the BDSM and the D/s lifestyle through online research. In self-examination, I discovered that I may very well be a submissive man. In the beginning, my knowledge of the lifestyle was rudimentary to say the least. I read how an actual D/s relationship truly worked in practice. It helped me realize that in my previous relationships I enjoyed doing the same things for a lady that a submissive man might do for a domme. While browsing the internet I discovered a website for a local maitresse. I sessioned with Miss Ann once a month and often discussed self-actualization. I had a basic understanding of the term, but I didn't realize she was translating her lessons to me as a submissive. After having many lengthy conversations on the topic and listening to her speak of her own actualization, I started to grasp the concept and related it to myself.
>
> What I eventually came to understand was I could actually feel comfortable being a male submissive. The stigma of being both a man and submissive is that of a weakling who

can't make decisions for himself. It always bothered and embarrassed me and caused me to stay in the shadows. I knew that for me being a submissive had nothing to do with being weak or unable to make decisions. Miss Ann's confidence sank in and I suddenly was comfortable with myself.

Letters of appreciation like the following reaffirmed my commitment and belief that my journey as a dominatrix was worthwhile and helping others.

You have my deepest admiration. I have not had the strength until now to even admit some of my fears, as well as some of my hidden desires. You are giving me the strength to venture into territory I would have never had the strength to venture and I thank you for all the help you are giving me in accepting who I am and what I feel inside.

I was touched by Sam's note and wrote him in return.

Your words make me so happy. I am directed by my mission statement and my manifesto to help direct individuals toward their own actualization. We cannot self-actualize in a closet of fear and shame.

There is NOTHING wrong with serving another person. Service is the backbone of D/s. In fact, I believe that those who serve are far stronger than those that are served. Macho guys have a lot to learn about the strength of the submissive male.

I believe that what you feel inside is your own psyche and inner voice speaking to you. Your own inner voice would not be nudging you if there was not something there that you need to explore. I believe that inner voice is the Universal God that resides within us all.

I would recommend that you find a femme domme guide and teacher that you respect and trust (a domme that has shown herself to be both accountable and trustworthy) to guide you.

Another sub wrote what he learned in his first session about the power of a trusting relationship.

Having arranged a meeting time during my phone interview, I arrived promptly at 2:00. Miss Ann answered the door and was a stunning portrait of a domme wearing tall spiked heels, black stockings, a short black skirt and a jacket that revealed awesome cleavage. Within a minute of my arrival I was on my knees kissing her feet, the proper way to greet a Queen. We then sat down and talked about what I was looking for as a sub and what she expected from me. Miss Ann was very warm and considerate and stressed that trust is the most important aspect of a Domme/sub relationship and I felt immediately that I could trust her.

Being relatively new to the scene I admit I was a bit nervous as Miss Ann led me down the steps to her very well-equipped dungeon, but I knew she wouldn't do anything to harm me. She instructed me to strip and went back upstairs. I did as I was told and waited, naked and exposed, for her to return. When she did, she began measuring me with a tape measure. Chest, legs, cock, I was going crazy wondering what was next! She asked me if I felt exposed before her and of course the answer was yes. She said I was about to be even more exposed and she was right! After being fitted with a collar I was put in my back on the bondage table and my arms and legs were suspended from the ceiling. As she inspected my cock she asked me if I had jacked off since we arranged the session. I had. She had ordered me not to and she could tell I had just by looking at my dick! She said she would deal with me later for that. She then left the room and came back with several items I couldn't see. But she did show me the shaving cream. And then she used it!

Humiliating? YES. But getting that much attention in that area of my body from such a Goddess was WORTH IT!

Miss Ann is truly a compassionate domme and knows instinctively what I need as a submissive and I look forward to serving her in the future. I'll just make sure I don't disobey her again!

The Yahoo! group forum continued to flourish as dozens of new members signed up daily. I spent several hours a day writing, approving essays others wrote and updating the forum. I was defining my holistic approach to domination. Subs seemed to love the rhetoric, photo content and trusted me. While online I parked my profile in the AOL Dominant Women chat room. This was primarily a linking mechanism to get the curious to join my Yahoo! group.

In its incubation, Dominant Women was a legitimate place for a domme and sub to foster a real life relationship. People took their roles seriously. At any given time, there were just as many dommes as subs in the chat room, all with different quirks. But as time passed, the room lost some of its sweetness and began to have the feel of a high school cafeteria. Egos got out of control and Dominant Women became like interactive reality TV.

Dommes who had been around for years didn't take kindly to my new age approach to domination with a philosophy and spiritual purpose. Some were jealous of the attention I was getting in the chat room. So I played the role of uppity domme, not letting their childish aggression affect me. SirSissy was a regular sub who took the role of chat room antagonist. He was an investment banker whose search for a domme worthy of his submission left him frustrated. He had found no match for his intellect. Sissy and I became partners-in-crime against the jealous dommes. We laughed at their posturing. Who could take them seriously?

Sissy began referring to these dommes as fat old cows which, of course, they detested. As a sub, Sissy had more control in Dominant Women than the dommes. He ran them ragged and they lost control of their demeanors every time he entered the chat room. Then he went over the top by typing, "M-o-o-o-o-o! I was hoping to find a real dominatrix in here, not a bunch of cows." That triggered an onslaught of angry chats. I watched the comedy scroll across the screen. It was all too much. Sissy roped me into his insults.

MistressHouston: I just wanted to say to the mouthy subs in here that I am not going to tolerate your behavior. Anyone who talks down to a domme isn't

worth a keystroke. sissy, do the world a favor and
put a gun to your head.

SirSissy: Houston, you are nothing more than a fraud.
I'd probably have to tell you what to do if I served
you. Miss Ann is the only real domme here. You'd be
lucky if she allowed you to touch her boots.

MistressHouston: HOW DARE YOU. You have no idea
who you are dealing with. Both of you will get what's
coming to you...

SirSissy: MOOOOOOOOO. You ready for milking, you
living, breathing sirloin to-be?

Sissy and I took the bovine insults up a notch and
started referring to the regulars as a herd of cows. We
chatted on the side and were in hysterics about how
childish online dommes were–not that we were any better.

SirSissy: What's new with The Herd today? M-o-o-o-o-o!
MistressHouston: F*ck you Sissy, you piece of sh*t
scum. You wouldn't last ten seconds in my dungeon
acting the way you do. If ann was a real Domme
she would come to your rescue and put you in your
place. That haughty b*tch thinks she can change the
world with her ridiculous mission. She should start by
teaching you some manners.

I found a picture of cows in a feedlot and decided
to have some fun on a free webpage builder, having no
clue the idea was going to get me into trouble. The Herd

homepage showed cattle at a trough with quote bubbles reading "moo" and "feed me." Over time the website evolved into an intricate parody loosely based on real life profiles and internet chat. I assigned mean-spirited spins on the dommes' names. MistressSatin became MistressFatten. We borrowed pictures of zoo animals and photoshopped hooves on dommes instead of boots. MistressMadeleine had a reputation as a hooker who sessioned in shabby motels, so I created an entire page featuring sleazy roadside motels at night. Her page read, "I'm MotelMaddy–ssshhhh, I'll meet you here."

Expanding the site by adding new pages every day became our obsession for a couple weeks. My favorite section was a long list of actual quotes snipped from the chat room. Sissy sent me an email with the best of them each day and I called my column Heard from the Herd. I put a Thomas Jefferson quote on the front page, beginning: "The only security of all is a free press." A footer on the page contained a disclaimer stating that The Herd was satire. But the dommes already hated us and when we unleashed The Herd website link in the chat room, we gave them good reason. All hell broke loose.

On May 8, 2003, I awoke to forceful knocks on my front door and went bleary-eyed to the door. Standing on my porch was crime beat reporter Jack Rinehart and a cameraman from WRTV 6. He waved a folder at me and said he had a police report that said I was operating a dungeon on the premises. He was doing a story whether or not I talked to him, he said, and claimed the police had a thick file they'd just sent downtown.

I felt as if concrete had just been poured around my feet. It looked as if the police had started an investigation I knew nothing about. Apparently, I had been outed.

"I have nothing to hide. But no cameras," I said.

> "Apparently the police had instigated an investigation. I felt as if concrete had just been poured around my feet. I had been outed.

Rinehart usually got leads from the police department, but in that instance he said a tip had been sent directly to him. I tried to explain my practice to Rinehart, talking to him like a kindergartner, but my work was too complicated for outsiders to understand in a single sound bite. I tried to cover my anxiety with unwavering poise. I even showed him my mission statement. Then the phone rang.

"It's probably a client," I said.

Rinehart asked if he could record.

"Audio only," I said.

He pulled out a tape recorder. After four rings I picked up the phone.

"Good morning."

My uninvited guests grinned.

"Yes, this is Miss Ann."

Most likely Rinehart's objective was to leave my house with something titillating. But the call was just to make an appointment, not anything weird or explicit. Afterward Rinehart asked to see my dungeon, which until then had been hidden from the general public. I made the cameraman leave his equipment upstairs and led the men downstairs. Their eyes adjusted to the night of the dungeon. Hanging on the wall were all of my implements–floggers, ball gags, restraints and masks, not to mention the whipping cross, bondage table, chains and steel cage.

"I bet it looks pretty creepy to you, doesn't it?" I said.

I pulled each implement down, one at a time, to demonstrate.

"A flogger can be used for tickling." I gently ran the flogger across the bondage table. "A blindfold intensifies a whisper. Restraint gives my client a sense of liberation when he's in the proper headspace. See? Nothing here is illegal. It's role-playing with props."

I explained the dungeon was a paradoxical world that would take someone unfamiliar with kink years to understand.

"Highly sophisticated people play these games," I said. "Their experience is exhilarating because their intellect is engaged."

Rinehart hadn't come to hear about fear liberation. His

cronies were probably waiting at the station to see what he bagged. As one who enjoyed control, I had zero. I felt helpless. He had ambushed my universe.

When the news van finally pulled away from the curb, I was shaken to the core. I had never been as paranoid or afraid in my life. My discreet practice was about to be on the eleven o'clock news. I needed to talk it out with someone who could steer me in the right direction, so I called the Fluttering Menace. I needed a strong ally and she was my best bet.

The Menace advised that I quickly get a strategy aligned and lay low until the broadcast aired. She gave me the names of two people: Sparrow, a major player in Indy's then small kink community, and Paul Pogue, an award-winning journalist with *NUVO,* a local alternative newspaper.

To prepare for the fallout, I called Sparrow and Pogue right away. Both of them said they would help with damage control but offered the same advice as the Menace–wait it out for the foreseeable future. Over the next week, I repressed my anxiety and hoped the story would go away, but I knew deep down it wouldn't. I even hid from my Yahoo! group. I usually penned multiple posts every day, but I couldn't harness the willpower to write anything except one short essay. I lived in a prison of my own thoughts, realizing my life was about to change forever.

All the while a buzz was developing about what Channel 6 would air. Radio stations ran promos featuring whips cracking and ghoulish sound effects. Someone called and said it was probably best if I didn't listen to the radio so I didn't. I pretended the story hadn't happened as I waited the six days with the rest of the city for the story to air on May 14. I was hoping for the best and expecting the worst. Sparrow invited me to the home she shared with her partner, a male dom, to watch the segment. I vigorously cleaned my house to pass the hours. At least I could return to an immaculate home when it was all over.

The Fluttering Menace had correctly pegged Sparrow as the person to see about being outed. She had founded Indy's only kink education organization, InKink, and was steering the group through its two-year qualifying period to become an official partner of the

NCSF–National Coalition for Sexual Freedom. The NCSF lobbied the media on personal freedoms and first amendment issues. Sparrow's kink organization held workshops throughout the year as a community education resource. Typical classes included topics ranging from proper flogging techniques to the therapeutic effects of aftercare.

I opted not to watch the Channel 6 newscast the night it aired. Afterward Sparrow told me the story was tabloid journalism but not as bad as I had feared. The police interviewed said they had no reason to believe I was doing anything illegal. The nearby school even sent notes home with students, telling parents my business wasn't a safety threat.

But the whole world knew my secret. My business had been exposed and I felt I was in trouble, yet an eerie calm came over me. Everything rode on how I handled communication from that point forward. Rather than get in a tizzy, I compartmentalized my fear and worked with my best foot forward. It was game time.

Within two hours of the broadcast, Sparrow had the NCSF's media liason on the phone. I was instructed to write a press release and publish it on my website. She gave me a template and said it was imperative I have the release ready by morning. Sparrow and I spent all night writing and editing. The press release read:

> Sometime prior to May 8, 2003, an anonymous tip was sent via the Internet to authorities and media services in Indianapolis, Indiana, including the Marion County Sheriff's Department, the Marion County Prosecutor's office, WRTV 6 News, and the *Indianapolis Star* newspaper. This email falsely alleged that a female Domina was offering extreme SM (sadomasochism), sexual services and nonconsensual activities in a residence located in a quiet, upscale Indianapolis neighborhood.

> On Thursday, May 8, 2003, WRTV 6 reporter Jack Rinehart made an unannounced visit to this resident with a cameraman stating he wanted to air the truth about what allegedly takes place at this residence. Stating she had nothing to hide, the resident agreed to be interviewed off camera to answer Mr. Rinehart's questions. Community education of the psychological power exchange known as D/s (Dominance/submission) is the basis of her small consulting business. She was led to believe her consent

to the interview would be an opportunity to further responsible awareness and education of her often misunderstood work.

Mr. Rinehart was informed that the mainstay of her work is imaginative theatrical role-play scenarios. He was also informed that there is no sexual contact allowed and 100% of her meetings are conducted with her wearing professional business attire. Further he was told that her clients are carefully screened through a detailed and lengthy telephone interview for which she charges a fee of $75.00. These interviews are critical, in that this is how she determines the real needs and motives of her potential clients. The interview also enables her to screen out uninformed potential clients who seek illegal sexually related services, which she clearly does not and will not provide.

The resident provided Mr. Rinehart with her mission statement, manifesto and an example of the simple contract that she uses with her clients, all of which plainly emphasize that her work does not involve sexual activities but rather focuses on a psychological power exchange based in a healthy dynamic. She provided Mr. Rinehart with the mission and manifesto statements that support her approach aimed to advance personal self-actualization as mirrored in Abraham Maslow's Hierarchy of Human Needs. She also indicated that another major aspect of her work is as a transformation artist and producer of photographic imagery with high visual impact.

In tandem with her mission to offer education to the community, she arranged permission for Mr. Rinehart to immediately contact Dr. Larry Davis, MD, a local psychiatrist/clinician, whose successful and long standing clinic is widely known for specializing in sex and gender related therapy. This clinic is located less than one mile from the television studio. No statement from this easily accessible and willing local expert was aired. Further, he aired no mention of her mission statement, manifesto or her work as a transformation artist, education consultant, and dominant guide in the frequently aired television and radio trailers or in the actual television broadcast.

Pogue came to Sparrow's to interview me two days after the broadcast and told me about sweeps week. Four times a year television stations measured what people were watching over a four-week period. In order to make themselves more valuable to advertisers, channels rolled out the most spectacular content they could find. In my case Rinehart didn't have any hard news. The police had already decided my activities were legal and Rinehart only had video footage of neighbors saying they had no idea what I was doing. I had been so intimidated by an investigative journalist shoving a camera in my face that I hadn't asked to examine the file and allowed Rinehart entrance because he said nothing would stop him from broadcasting. But the truth was, the Meridian-Kessler dominatrix was a non-story. I had been manipulated into opening my dungeon to public view.

Paul Pogue had his angle on my story immediately. He passed no judgment and every question was direct and respectful during the three-hour interview. Pogue told me the folder Rinehart had waved in my face contained a closed file outlining my actions as legal. There never had been any pending police action. His story in *NUVO* came out a week after the newscast and set the record straight, questioning the journalistic integrity of the news station. Rinehart didn't even return his calls requesting an interview.

The *NUVO* article also quoted Jim Shasky, an Emmy award-winning director/producer and professor of telecommunications. His opinion was that Rinehart was making news rather than covering it. He said news was supposed to be accurate and if it wasn't, then it was entertainment.

The damage control strategy the Menace and Sparrow helped hatch was a home run. I immediately circulated the *NUVO* article and linked it from my website so the public would be able to see the other side of the story. A weight lifted off my shoulders after Pogue's humanizing story was published.

When a D/s lifestyle pal from Cincinnati named Arie heard the internet rave, he instructed me to pack my bags, lock the house and indulge in a worry-free long weekend in the Queen City. He wasn't taking no for an answer because he knew I was rattled to the core. He promised to spoil me and let me breathe. The same day, I packed a suitcase, fueled up the Altima and embarked on the easy two-hour drive to refuge.

As I turned onto Arie's street, I saw a church sign that read, "The darkest hour is often the shadow of the wing of God." Another coincidence? The chemical rush I felt was all too familiar. I exhaled. It would all be fine in the end.

"Through the Indiana secretary of state's office records, MistressTrish traced a corporation name I had used to register a domain. She then had my home address and publicized my location online in Dominant Women.

When I returned to Indianapolis, the energy of my home was dead. I felt displaced. My phone was quiet because my clients must have been spooked. Were they afraid my lines were tapped? That someone would spy on them? My closest subs came out of the woodwork with encouragement, but business slowed to a halt. It was just me and the cats in my big house.

Then SirSissy forwarded me the email that MistressHouston had sent out. The content was, of course, fabricated, absurd and libelous. She had instructed an army of dommes called the Responsible Dominant Women of

AOL to forward the release to every government and media entity with a searchable email address. And the dommes didn't just press send once. Other local media had ignored the far-fetched attack but Channel 6 ran with it.

PRESS RELEASE FROM MISTRESSHOUSTON

Subject: One of many handed directly to Indianapolis covert vice.

Location Of Investigated Party: Indianapolis, panders and commits solicitation of prostitution in Indianapolis, Indiana and Chicago, Illinois with "stable" of prostitutes.

Sex Of Person In Question: Questionable Female, may be a crossdresser.

Occupation Of Individual: Runs "The Reformatory" in Indianapolis, Indiana.

Registration Address Of Website By Said Party: www.thereformatory.com

Actual Home Address Of Said Party: [redacted] Finances and runs a home of ill repute, consisting of a man-made dungeon where lewd acts of bondage and other fetish events are sold for sexual deviates. Has several assistants of whom she solicits sex and degrading events for as well. Complaints by paying clients for trade of sex are that the house madam commits live endangering scenarios and has a history of criminal behavior.

Biography Of Miss Ann From Persons Online And Off: Ms. Ann is a menace to society and well known among the entire b/d and s/m societies of America Online.

The individual disregarded the "safe word" (a code used for a submissive when he is saying enough is enough) and endangering a man's life and literally committing a felony. The individual in question took the situation beyond an erotic encounter but to the lowest depths and endangered someone's life. Putting that poor man/sub into a real life "Helter Skelter" and almost murdering him, literally. The situation is beyond what is acceptable in any alternative lifestyle "dungeon," private "scene" or by any professional "dominatrix." The issue is of concern for the general public as she poses a threat to the well being of the Indianapolis and Chicago communities as a whole. It is the Indianapolis Police, State Police and Mental Health department's civic duty to investigate these allegations and protect the city as a whole. Any person visiting this legalized bordelo consisting of prostitute co-workers also into this lifestyle would be putting his very life in jeopardy.

An Embarrassment To The City Of Indianapolis:
She is an embarrassment to the city of Indianapolis. Included is an image of her in a public park full of children in the afternoon playing. If you view the images, you will note that a man in full latex drag clothing is behind her on a leash wearing stilleto high heels and more. She's a threat to society as a whole. What does the picture of her in front of kids with a sub on a leash wearing latex? It says "I am a mental and have no limits. It is probable that I was raised by a family with no values, it has not registered to me that I am not normal and acceptable by society doing this."

She took a stiletto submissive crossdresser in a latex hood on a leash through a park in broad daylight in the morning in front of kids playing. You don't take that

around kids it's equivalent to child molesting . . . you
mess with children's heads doing something like this.
It is not right and a judge in a court of law would say
the same thing, police would say the same thing, social
workers would say the same thing and so would clergy.
Not only is it cruelty to children, it disturbs the peace,
violates the law and it's also indecent exposure.

A Molester Of Childrens' Minds:
There is a place and time for everything and that park
in daytime was not a fetish ball: that was a park full of
children and elderly innocent people. Look at that guy in
heels at the park if I had my kids on the swings I would
have beat him senseless. Everyone does not need to
KNOW what Melyssa does at her house. She however
thinks they do! She needs a padded cell for raping the
minds of children in a public park like that in a public
display. It should be a felony since she has no respect
for the law whatsoever or people.

MistressHouston's press release was just the first step
in an effort to destroy me. Next, she created a website
called The Sinister Life Online and Offline of America's
Most Insane and Dangerous Dominatrix. The site claimed
I was a serial killer, a sociopath and a stalker. She wrote
the world was laughing at Indianapolis because it couldn't
cage me in a padded cell and compared me to the Glenn
Close character in *Fatal Attraction*.

Houston sent her new website link to every domme and
sub who entered the Dominant Women chat room, just
like Sissy and I had done with The Herd. Subs hated the

mudslinging. They wanted all the dommes to peacefully coexist. The more time we spent fighting, the less attention they received. The petty melodrama ensued.

I was aware that The Herd website would ruffle feathers and I'd expected pushback, but never in a million years would I have guessed that what was happening in Dominant Women could manifest itself in real life. Eventually I found out who was behind MistressHouston's internet assault.

A domme named MistressTrish had a personal grudge against me because of a trip I took to Seattle to visit a mutual friend named Droid. MistressTrish and Droid were beginning a real life D/s relationship but Droid lacked confidence and asked me for advice online. As I counseled him, we became friends. One day he suggested I fly out to Seattle for a short vacation but when he was upfront and told Trish, she got jealous. She forbade me to go to Seattle and emailed incessantly, warning me to keep my hands off her man. It was an unfortunate misunderstanding but I wasn't going to stay home on account of it.

The trip sealed my friendship with Droid but Seattle had its price. When my holiday was over, MistressTrish made me her target. Within days of my return, she busied herself digging to find something to crush me. Through the Indiana secretary of state's office records, she traced a corporation name I had used to register a domain. MistressTrish then had my home address and publicized my location online in Dominant Women, making sure

MistressHouston saw it. The two dommes thought outing me would teach me a lesson.

With business stalled, I decided to apply for a home equity loan and shut down for three months to renovate my house. I hired a guy to remove the carpet, refinish the hardwood, lay tile in the sunroom, remove layers of wallpaper and repaint interior walls. I planned to live inconspicuously under construction as my story faded from public scrutiny.

Overseeing the renovations made me stir-crazy so I occupied myself with activities that would advance my interest in personal freedom. I knew about the Libertarian Party from old friends who were members but I had never studied its tenets. I found the Libertarian Party platform online. Its preamble covered three main areas: protection of the sovereign individual, first amendment freedom, and fiscal responsibility and restriction of government power in favor of the free market.

I was already a libertarian and didn't realize it! I sent in thirty dollars to join. A week later I got a wallet-sized plastic card in the mail with the party's statement of principles. "We hold that all individuals have the right to exercise sole dominion over their own lives, and have the right to live in whatever manner they choose, so long as they do not forcibly interfere with the equal right of others to live in whatever manner they choose."

Consent was at the core of being a Libertarian, just like D/s. When the party hired a new state development coordinator, Robert Butler, the following week, I phoned him to volunteer my services. I even told him about being outed in the media as a dominatrix and he still accepted my offer. Robert was planning a tour of the entire state to introduce himself to each county's party chairman and hear its fundraising plans as well as try to attract new party members. I offered to document his travels with my digital camera. My schooling in libertarian politics began on the road and my new political home felt just right. Thanks to Robert's tutelage.

By October, my house renovations were complete and Rinehart's story had put me back on the radar of friends I hadn't seen over the last two years. In a weird way my outing ended up being a blessing in disguise. My old roommate Keith said the grapevine was buzzing with talk about Mely, the dominatrix. Everybody was dying for gossip. I had an idea to bring us all together again by the one thing I did best–throw a legendary party. I quickly designed and printed postcard invitations. Then just after I had mailed fifty invites to friends, I received a phone call from my Aunt Paula.

"You need to drop everything and drive to Georgia to see your grandma," she said.

I told her I couldn't leave town just then. Business had resumed and I had a full schedule of clients plus the party was coming up.

"No, Mely. You have to leave right now. She's in the hospital."

I made arrangements with pigtails to watch the house and packed a suitcase. My Uncle David lived in the same town as Grandma and acted as her caretaker. He offered me a place to stay. The moment I walked into her hospital room and saw Grandma in bed, my eyes welled up.

"Poor old Grandma doesn't have long for this world," she said just as I said to her when I was five.

We both started laughing and spent the next three days talking. She told stories about her life before I was born and we talked about her one true love, her second husband. The man I knew as Grandpa had passed away when I was twelve. We reminisced over my first lessons in sales, tagging along as she peddled make-up and hygiene products door-to-door in the poor parts of Palmerton. I thanked her for instilling the love of Jesus in me. Grandma's Jesus wasn't a mega church or holy roller Jesus. Hers was a pure consciousness of Christ that she lived every day.

"I don't want to die, Mely," she said.

"As long as I'm alive, you're alive in me." Uttering those words filled me with joy and relief.

Aunt Paula came to the hospital on my last day and handed the nurse a camera. That photo still sits on a sill in my kitchen. I was heartbroken, driving back to Indy because I knew I'd seen my grandma for the last time. Her values and strength would live on in me, but knowing she was going to die filled me with sadness.

I came right back to the busy schedule I'd put on hold. Without any delay, my old friend Radford called about the party because he'd already signed up for an annual Halloween party bus equipped with booze and a driver to escort costumed bar-hoppers around the city. He thought what better party to crash than one with a bona fide dungeon?

"Would it be cool if I brought a busload of people with me?" he asked.

"The more the merrier!" I said.

"Are the freaks going to be there?"

He was, of course, referring to kinky people–subs and all. I understood my more conventional pals might be perturbed by the D/s crowd, but I never discriminated against anyone. Plus it was Halloween and the freaks were coming out for my extravaganza.

My subs decorated the porch with cobwebs and set up a fog machine in the front yard. When guests arrived, they were greeted by a disembodied head–a sub who had consented to crouch under a card table with a hole cut in it. I'd painted REDRUM on the stairs. A spread of canapes including my cream cheese torte covered in black and orange caviar was laid out in the sunroom.

Radford dressed as a televangelist and had purple-haired Tammy Faye Baker with him. My good friend Uncle Barry, sipped a cocktail in the sunroom. Everyone who mattered to me was under my roof. Not only was my house renovated, but so was I. It didn't take long for the party to make its way to the basement. One of my high school friends was awestruck by the detail of the dungeon.

"Wow, Mely! You really go all out for Halloween." Apparently she hadn't heard the news about my lifestyle.

Explaining to my guests how each implement in the dungeon worked was a lot more fun than the last time I gave a lesson to outsiders. With subs happy to volunteer, I demonstrated some light spanking and flogging and even showed off my sexy leather suspension restraints by hoisting a sub's arms and legs in the air. My guests seemed fascinated and were not ill at ease. People imbibed, laughed and caught up on life. Like the old days, the late-nighters wound up on the veranda and talked the night away.

Grandma's funeral was on the last day of the year. Uncle David, who was an ordained minister with his own church, organized her funeral arrangements. The day after I heard the news, I called him.

"Uncle David, can I have five minutes to say a few words at the service?"

"Oh, Mely, what are you going to do?"

"You've got nothing to worry about. God told me to and I need to follow through."

The day of the funeral, I took the podium, determined not to cry.

Eulogy for Grandma

For years I thought today would be the most impossibly sad, devastating and difficult day of my life. I've always dreaded the physical death of my grandmother.

In fact, I've said many times the day Grandma dies, I'll be a bona fide basket case. However, I have learned fear is always smoke.

At a young age I understood she was the person who would give me wisdom. I was afraid she would leave this planet before she could impart her knowledge to me. Grandma has a big light. Grandma lit that light every single day she lived. Even on the days when the light was small, she shared it. On the days it was big, many hungry souls nourished on her love.

Everyone wants to be accepted one hundred percent for who they are without judgment. This lesson was not taught only by words. I received the lesson from Grandma by her deeds and actions.

Through countless hours selling cosmetics with her in Palmerton, Grandma was my very first sales mentor. Her approach showed meeting human need was more important than money. She earned a living and made a difference in the daily lives of her clients. I will always live by that lesson.

No matter the crazy difficulty I went through growing up, Grandma was my rock. I ran to her to find comfort, encouragement and most importantly acceptance of who I am no matter what. She always greeted me with open arms.

My grandmother was and is the single most profound influence and person in my life. I feel particularly blessed to have endured such a significant amount of time with her. Those of you who knew her from more of a distance could not help but be radiated in light from knowing her.

All this talk about the past leads me to the present and the future. Right now we're basking in the great love that was and is Grandma.

I have a challenge for everyone here: Will you all carry forth the torch that burned so bright in her?

Each of us has an opportunity to do so in our own way, true to who we are as individuals and free of judgment.

In the spirit of free will, we can carry on in the very same light that burned inside of Grandma.

Because her light lives in me, I have a true sense of joy, not sadness. I believe Grandma wants us to laugh and enjoy each other. Let's celebrate and live fully in light, shall we? If we do so, her light in us will always stay alive.

December 31, 2003

After I spoke these words, my uncle took the podium while putting a piece of paper back into his pocket.

He then said, "I had prepared something but there is not anything else that needs said."

Chapter Ten

The night of my Halloween party, I opened my big mouth and agreed to plan a costume party for a thousand people. What was I thinking? I'd never done anything on that scale before. The next day I woke up in a panic, unaware, of course, that the experience was going to prepare me to plan another kind of party in the near future. A tea party.

Halloween night an artist friend named Alex implored me to take over the upcoming tenth anniversary Erotic Arts Show. He'd done it for nine years and no longer had time to do all the organizing. Alex had put on the first show in 1994 to give local artists an outlet for displaying erotic work they normally weren't able to exhibit. I'd met Alex at the 1997 Erotic Arts Show for which I had made the salmon mousse lady.

"The only condition, Mely," he said, "is this has to be the grandest, most extravagant erotic art show this town has ever seen."

I had no template for throwing a party on the scale Alex described. But I needed some success to boost my self-esteem after my recent experiences. I wanted recognition and respect from people in the arts and kink communities. Overcompensating by jumping in over my head was something I'd done in the past, and I'd just said yes again. Then I calmed down and I told myself, it will work out in the end. It always does. I had a full year to turn it into the most memorable Erotic Arts Show ever. Piece of cake!

I quickly figured out that the expenses would be daunting. There was the thousand dollars for the twenty-four-hour venue rental, printing programs and tickets, curator fee, cash prizes for the art competition, booking a DJ and bands, setting up a stage with sound and lighting, security, plus hundreds of small incidentals I wouldn't know about until I was in it. I changed the event name to a more elegant sounding banner, the Erotic Arts Ball, wanting to give the perception that this wasn't a raunchy affair. It was to be a serious art competition. The bar was set. The show had to be beautiful and garner good press from local art critics.

I booked a sublime two-story gothic church, a national historic landmark in Fountain Square. The first story was an ideal space to hang art and the second story housed the original cathedral with a forty-foot arched ceiling, stained glass windows, a stage at one end and choir balcony at the other. The stage was perfect for performance art and the balcony was great for the DJ. The venue owner also allowed me to use the basement, so I decided to install a BDSM dungeon and tables for vendors to peddle their kinky wares.

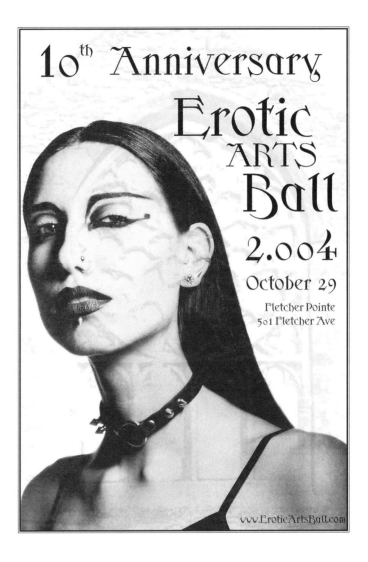

For the kinksters at the party, the downstairs dungeon playspace would be a major draw. The Fluttering Menace offered to be the ball's dungeon monitor. Having a competent dungeon master was as necessary as having a lifeguard at a swimming pool. The Menace not only pledged to ensure public safety but would also lend equipment to furnish the playspace.

Next I needed an image so tantalizing that people would commit months in advance to attend. Enter Prissy, my Madison Avenue graphic designer with whom I'd worked for three years. She created my international dominatrix ads and my first logo. We got busy online and she quickly created the iconic image that sold the ball.

Then another idea occurred to me. Who said it had to cost more to be a VIP? That launched a ticket sale campaign publicizing the event had a capacity for only a thousand guests. By capping the guest list at a thousand, expectations were in place. I had decided to sell the first hundred tickets with VIP privileges at a discount. VIPs could preview the art at a champagne reception before doors opened. Cheaper but more exclusive. Five hundred tickets were sold in advance.

Jennifer Kaye curated a local gallery and agreed to hang the show. We hammered out entry guidelines, artwork requirements and deadlines. She helped me understand how to conceptualize the orchestration of a serious juried exhibit. I needed a judge with great credentials and asked Dr. Frédéric Allamel, PhD in the sociology of arts and architecture, from the Sorbonne. He wrote a book on the erotic art and artifact collections of Dr. Alfred Kinsey at the Kinsey Institute at Indiana University. Months earlier Dr. Allamel inquired about my D/s practice and requested a meeting to discuss my private dungeon and photograph it for a manuscript he was writing about erotic architecture. With his soft French accent, black cashmere turtleneck he wore that day, and tousled gray hair, he was one of the most elegant men I'd ever met.

Jennifer told me about a fast-track cultural tourism grant to be given by the Indianapolis Arts Council. The grant would provide up to five thousand dollars for projects of cultural significance to the city. I saw the ball as an opportunity to elevate Indianapolis to the level of other cities on the erotic arts circuit. Most major cultural centers in the US and Europe had fetish or erotic arts events with attendance into the thousands. London had the Rubber Ball, New York had the Black & Blue Ball, New Orleans gave the Memnoch Ball and San Francisco, the Folsom Street Fair.

Mayor Bart Peterson spoke often about his vision to remake Indianapolis into a world class city. We already had a new football stadium, a renovated and expanded convention center, future plans for a Super Bowl bid and the rebranding of our cultural arts districts. Progress had been made in distinguishing Indy from little more than a transportation hub in the middle of bean and cornfields, but from an arts standpoint, there was still room for improvement. I worked hard on the grant application then found out before I'd even sent it in that our event was going to be turned down. The idea was rejected in advance and there was nothing I could do but spend less.

The dress code was formal, erotic or costume. Everything from street clothes and tuxedos to electrical tape across nipples was accepted attire. The big night of the ball, costumes were gorgeous, the fetish attire tasteful and fun. The crowd put their best selves forward, carrying themselves in a sophisticated and civilized manner. It was great to see friends coming together for the cause. Connie Ziegler, a local historian and vintage shop owner, stood at a microphone and educated the audience on the history of undergarments while models walked the catwalk, clad in negligees, open-bottom girdles, bullet bras, garters and stockings.

Another friend enlisted a troupe and choreographed sexy yoga moves to music and performed during the art reception. Rachael of Surrean Designs, a local custom corset-maker, volunteered to put on a fashion show with a theatrical performance. Her models acted out naughty nursery rhyme vignettes in her corsetry. Radford lent himself to the role of emcee for the evening and dazzled the audience with his booming voice.

Uncle Barry purchased virtual reality googles for patrons to see themselves getting flogged or spanked. Perhaps the over-the-top act was Trigger, the Human Equine. Trigger, the man with the soul of a horse, had appeared in documentaries that explored his unusual lifestyle. Any woman at the ball who wanted a ride could sit on his custom-made shoulder saddle and guide him with the reins and bit in his mouth.

Rachael sewed a fabulous satin gown as a gift for me. It had a plunging neckline that wrapped around my waist and sleeves and hem embellished with dangling amber-colored glass beads. I also wore an amber ring and a crystal pendant necklace. For me, the evening was like a blur. I was too busy being the point person, solving every problem that arose, to slow down and enjoy the festivities, but people really came out of the woodwork for the ball and that made me proud.

My guests gathered as I took the microphone and recited Marianne Williamson's words about liberation from fear. She had written that when we free ourselves of our fear, our presence helps others to also feel free. When I finished, my guests burst into cheers and a loud ovation. It was a glorious moment.

ChapterEleven

I had accomplished everything I wanted with the Erotic Arts Ball. *NUVO* and *INtake,* an offshoot of the *Indianapolis Star,* both raved about the elegance of the event and the fearless inhibitions of our well-behaved crowd. When I first started working on the ball, I received an email from MistressHouston, congratulating me on overcoming the obstacles I had faced and for putting on the Erotic Arts Ball. She empathized with me and fingered the other dommes as the ones who had outed me. It seemed they had turned on her as well.

I could have told her to screw off, but I'd softened toward her and the people who had turned against me. Having taken down The Herd website the year before, I'd been content to move beyond the online nonsense. I was in a place where past drama didn't affect me anymore. Why should I stay mad? In a weird way, the hurdles I had jumped over had put me in my current position. It was a blessing in disguise. I let bygones be bygones.

I lay low with a companion to distract me during the months following the ball. Ted was the offbeat musical genius who had created the soundtrack for the ball's reception. He helped me recharge my batteries before my next project–a retail boutique to open in the spring of 2005. I didn't know exactly how I was going to accomplish it but that had not stopped me from announcing it in the Erotic Arts Ball program. In my mind, it was the next logical step in my career.

Without much of a business plan, I figured I could eventually replace my session revenue stream with retail profit. I envisioned a place that kept normal hours where people could come to talk, buy wares and attend educational forums. I didn't think it through much more than that. I was high off the success of the ball and idealistic. But first, I needed a rest so I took my session calendar down several notches and kept my schedule light.

When I was ready to work again, I scouted all over the northside and downtown for a storefront to lease. Turning up nothing, I called Uncle Barry to ask for advice. He suggested a space he had open downtown at the Chatham Center. He could knock down the wall between two art studios to create a large retail space. It would be cheap and I didn't have to sign a lease. He must have known my plan was half-baked.

Within a couple weeks, Uncle Barry started work to open up the space. To transform it, I had to peel up the vinyl floor tiles, repair and paint the walls, install lighting and find retail display furnishings. Needing help, I put a call out in the kink community for volunteers. Many extra hands enlisted, young adults who wanted to be part of the scene and showed up every day to assist with the cosmetic renovations. I could only pay them with lunch and steep discounts on store items. Within a few weeks the boutique was ready to furnish.

I placed a large order with a company in England for latex gloves, stockings, bustiers, garter belts, panties and dresses. American companies furnished my leather collars, leashes, whips, restraints and floggers. I wanted to stock a quality selection for every kind of shopper, whether it be a sexy outfit, European seamed stockings, bondage gear or role-play toys. Male chastity devices were in relatively large demand but no retail outlet in Indiana carried them, so I stocked up. By the time I completed my inventory buys, I had the entire gamut of BDSM and D/s role-play gear. The photographer from the Erotic Arts Ball consigned dungeon furniture, including an impressive St. Andrew's cross, that gave the inventory broader appeal to serious lifestyle dominants and submissives.

Part of my plan was to make the boutique double as an art gallery featuring erotic works by local artists. I started lining up artists to freshen my walls with new pieces every couple of months. In the end my wares, while kinky, were not legally classified as adult retail because I did not sell insertables or pornography. I was allowed by law to carry up to twenty-four percent of my inventory as items that could be construed as adult, though I marketed my boutique as a unique niche in an untapped kinky marketplace.

The evening before opening to the public, I offered an invitation-only preview in my Yahoo! group so members could have first dibs. That night an awkward young bondage freak showed up. Justin fit the mold of guys I met through the years who weren't okay with themselves as submissives.

"Never forget you are special," I told him as I bagged his purchases.

Justin needed encouragement even more than I understood. In his wrinkled plaid shirt and bad haircut, he was a certified mess. I didn't think he had a real friend in the world.

He appeared at the shop again on his day off and told me he took care of his elderly aunt and worked nights at a box store. He was sweet but seemed to live a life with little joy and I saw an opportunity to help him explore his true self as sub.

"I need my caffeine fix. Would you go get me a large coffee?" I asked.

When he returned, he didn't seem to want to leave so we talked awhile about his kinky interests. That was when I learned he had done self-bondage for years without a play partner.

"How would you like to help out at the shop?" I asked.

"Do you mean it?"

"It would be a godsend to me and let you get more involved in the scene."

That was how Justin entered into my service. Before long, he started showing up every day he had off and before his shifts. I had him clean the adjacent art gallery and vacuum the public spaces of the building for Uncle Barry, too. Justin was practically giddy to serve as a submissive for the first time in his life. The first step toward bringing him out of his shell was to help him feel better about his looks so I told him to get new glasses and wear only black trousers and shirts. I also recommended a stylist on nearby Mass Ave to fix that bowl cut.

The leather training collar he wore at the shop gave Justin a sense of belonging to someone and something bigger than himself and in the months to come, I would watch him overcome his awkwardness. He seemed most at home when I bound and locked him in the giant birdcage in the middle of the boutique.

The grand opening took place a couple of months after business was in full swing. I booked a popular local band, Lunar Event, to play in the main gallery while guests enjoyed champagne, sparkling water, chocolates and caviar torte. About seventy-five people from my private email list showed up to help me celebrate. It was gratifying to see our whole tight-knit kink scene in attendance. The boutique acted as a de facto kink headquarters in Indy. Sparrow, the Fluttering Menace, artists from the Erotic Arts Ball and major players from my past all were in good spirits and promoting each other's work at the gathering. We were brothers and sisters in this small, peculiar society, harmoniously working together and supporting one another.

"During the previous two decades, the gay community had worked to build acceptance and political clout. I hoped to help build the same acceptance for the kink community.

Meanwhile, I rarely scheduled sessions but chose to spend more time on the retail business, hosting discussion groups and lending my time to an emerging monthly fetish party at a downtown nightclub. I was becoming more involved in Indy's now official NCSF affiliate, InKink. During my media outing two years earlier, Sparrow had been in the process of bringing this group into the national coalition. Our new status meant more power to implement strategies for overcoming injustices against people who engaged in alternative sexual lifestyles and relationships. Had it not been for Sparrow's support in the wake of Rinehart at my door, my side of the story would likely not have been told.

As repayment, I gave Sparrow a free table at the Erotic Arts Ball to assist InKink's fundraising and donated an autographed out-of-print photography book to their auction. They raised about a thousand dollars that night. However, InKink membership had dwindled to a small number. Sparrow was burned out and wanted to step down, having worked for years promoting InKink. I knew how important our NCSF affiliation was in the long run, that there was power in numbers, and we needed to stick together to be heard. But with so few members and no forthcoming leadership, the group could fall apart.

During the previous two decades, I'd watched how the gay community LGBT (lesbian, gay, bi-sexual, transgendered) had worked to build acceptance and political clout. Politicians had even begun to ride in their parades to show support. I hoped to help build the same acceptance for the kink community. We needed five members for the next year's board. I was willing and so was Liza, the young domme who once worked in my dungeon. I recruited two more and the Fluttering Menace also agreed to serve. Next on the agenda, we had to increase membership and our bank account, so I proposed that my boutique become an official partner of InKink and offer a ten percent store discount to new members. I then sold enough new memberships to add a thousand dollars to the club's checking account.

A few weeks after I opened the shop, a college student named Janet from the kink goth crowd decided to put on a monthly fetish party at a downtown club. She asked if I would help promote it through my Yahoo! group and among shoppers. InKink would have an information table at the event and I could set up a small retail display. The Menace was going to run the slave auction, which always livened up a party and helped people interact. Once purchased, a slave had to oblige his or her new owner's desires for the evening. Typical demands were fetching drinks, foot rubs and holding doors. At one auction, I purchased a pretty girl and gave her a bottle of perfumed water, instructing her to mist me whenever I felt overheated.

The night of the party, I closed up shop early and drove to the venue with retail display grid wall packed in the backseat and boxes of gear and InKink literature in my trunk. About a half a dozen people were outside, congregated near the door.

"Weren't we supposed to be here at eight?" one said.

"Where's Janet?" I asked.

"She's not here yet," Sparrow said.

"What? Where is she? This is her party!" I was annoyed.

Janet didn't arrive for an hour and a half and about twenty people later. I blew up and told her she was being unprofessional, that the person in charge had to be on time. Maybe I was too rough on Janet but she had kept everyone waiting and I'd closed early to be on time. We all went in and I began to hastily set up my display. The

186

Fluttering Menace came by and complained that the InKink table wasn't set up. When I suggested somewhat impolitely that she help me out, she walked off with her chin in the air. I had no idea that little fracas was going to have consequences.

As the auction was about to start, I noticed an elegant looking man in an impeccable Armani suit, a highly unusual sight for this crowd. He was having a drink with a male friend at the bar so I walked over. "I don't know about you gentlemen, but I intend to purchase some human flesh tonight," I said in a dramatic tone and put some cash on the bar.

"I'm Derek. And I'm interested," he said. "How does this work?"

Just standing next to him made me feel more alive. I wanted to know him and I wanted him to touch me. I told him to pull out his wallet and feel free to bid on any property he wanted. The Fluttering Menace took the stage and called up the first sub, a pale, skinny kid with red hair.

"Here we have Jon," she said. "The bidding starts at one dollar."

"I've got one dollar," someone said in the back.

"Two dollars!" another woman said.

"I've got ten bucks for him!" I shouted.

"Sold to Miss Ann for ten dollars!"

The room cheered and the atmosphere livened. Derek purchased a pretty young lass and focused on her for the rest of the night. However, I spied him watching me and sensed alchemy. I purchased three more geeky guys and eventually made them crawl on the floor behind me like ducklings following their mama, a display of humiliation. At the end of the night, I said goodbye to Derek and handed him my business card, hoping I'd see him again.

A few days later Derek arrived unannounced at the boutique with a bottle of good vintage Port and paté de foie gras. I closed up and invited him to the gallery lounge across the hall from my shop. As we talked, I knew he was dominant and that I would yield to him. It surprised me that I liked feeling submissive around him. For the first time since I had begun D/s, I had met a dom I wanted to be intimate with.

Just as a romance began with Derek, a storm was brewing right under my nose at InKink. As the next meeting began, Liza announced that InKink would not be invited back to the fetish party because I hadn't set up the information table as promised. The Fluttering Menace demanded to know why I had sold gear from my shop instead of setting up for InKink. I tried to explain about the time crunch and bickering ensued. As the meeting ended, the Menace asked if I was feeling well and said my memory lapse could indicate a medical condition. She said instability was unbecoming in a dominant and I might not be competent to represent InKink. I had seen this dynamic once before during the chat room fiasco and couldn't believe it was happening again in a group I had supported and helped grow.

"We're going to look at this situation very closely, Miss Ann," the Menace said. I was tired of dealing with petty dissension. The first step in advancing kinky people's status in society was to stop fighting among ourselves Gays had changed their sexual minority into an organized faction by coming together as citizens. *After the Ball–How America Will Conquer Its Fear and Hatred of Gays in the 90's*, a book written by two Harvard grads, Marshall Kirk and Hunter Madsen, laid out a plan for unity and media publicity that gays would use to prove they weren't just an avoidable subculture. We could use a version of their ideas to help kinky people validate themselves as a community. Through improved citizenship and charity, we could be seen as a viable group of self-respecting people who were making a difference.

When the Responsible Dominant Women of AOL had sent my address to the police and news media, I overcame the consequences with my head held high and didn't retaliate. But having close associates in real life try to besmirch my good name crossed the line. I wasn't going to let Liza and the Menace sabotage me. First, I needed to investigate what was really happening. I found out from Janet that she had said nothing about kicking InKink out of future parties. I wrestled with what to do, knowing I didn't have long before Liza and the Menace aligned themselves to throw me off the InKink board. All they needed was one more vote and they would have a three-to-two majority.

After putting so much effort into breathing a second life into InKink, I began to wonder if the negative gossip I'd heard over the years was true. Long-standing members had told me stories about the cliquey nature of InKink and how they ostracized people who weren't in their inner circle. It sounded like herd behavior. Perhaps because I was trying to do something different, I was viewed as an outsider.

I decided to end their game by refunding memberships because I could no longer support InKink. I had to tread lightly, though. All the major players in D/s were connected, and making a move that could undermine an established group had to be executed with prudence. Before acting, I wanted the blessing of a domme who carried more weight than the rest us put together.

A godfather-like figure named Katrianna reigned over the old guard Master/slave scene in a five-state area and was far more disciplined and respected than any other domme in the Midwest. She was well schooled in the traditions and protocols set forth by the oldest Master/slave societies in the US and Europe. Her D/s practices were much more intense and profound than mine. Rather than give subs two-hour sessions, Katrianna was a TPE (Total Power Exchange) domme. In a TPE relationship, the sub turned all his power over to a master and in return the master controlled all decisions in the sub's life. Katrianna saw her subs as consenting property. The master cared for and protected her sub, referred to as slave, and made sure he was never in harm's way. Katrianna had practiced TPE for many years.

Unexpectedly one afternoon, Katrianna dropped by the boutique to look around. I felt honored and a few days later called her about my plan. I wanted to show respect and get her nod before making my move. And I might need a future ally. The Menace had once called the police on Katrianna. Problem was, Katrianna was already so networked that rather than cause a stir at her door, the police told her who had called them. Katrianna let it go as if nothing had happened. She was wise enough to know that enemies either devised the path of their own undoing or someone else would come along and do it for them.

"I need to talk with you about a problem," I told her later over the phone. "I hope you can give me some counsel."

"I'm listening," Agatha said.

"I hate melodrama but it's about the Menace."

"What has she done this time?"

I explained that she was spreading rumors about me because of what had happened at the fetish party.

"Sounds like something the Menace would do," she said.

"They're wrangling to oust me, Katrianna," I said. "And the most absurd part is that a lot of new members signed up at my shop. I'm the main reason the membership grew but now, the backstabbing could ruin my business."

Katrianna asked me what I planned to do and I told her about the refund idea.

"I don't think it's unethical and you know how I feel," she said. "Do what you must."

After saying goodbye to Katrianna, I worried if I could afford to refund twenty-five dollars to fifty people. Not really. But the consequences of doing nothing were too much to risk. I needed to make sure I came up unscathed.

I drafted my apology with a brief explanation to the members, saying The Reformatory backed what it sold. I went on to say that they could follow their conscience and stay in the group or leave. If anyone wanted a refund, I would give them cash, no questions asked. In the end I gave back three hundred twenty-five dollars, money well spent. After that, the group dwindled and within a few months was defunct and along with it, the NCSF coalition partnership I had wanted to protect.

ChapterTwelve

As if that was not enough, trouble was brewing between Uncle Barry and the local neighborhood association and daycare center across the street, from The Reformatory Boutique. When the art gallery had closed, Uncle Barry leased the space to a small theater troupe.The first thing they did was cover the large front windows with black plastic which raised suspicions in the neighborhood. The daycare center director thought the blackout meant something nefarious was going on and after seeing my ad in NUVO, she got on the phone and got busy calling the neighborhood association.

"The windows belong to those theater kids!" I said.

"I know," Uncle Barry replied. "The real problem is that part of the property is being used for retail." Barry assured me he was running interference and I should lay low but I was hearing the beat of political war drums. This time not just dommes on the rampage but a group with real power. He suggested I allow some people from the neighborhood association into my shop to let them see that nothing illegal was going on. Maybe we could get a few neighbors in our corner.

Three people, including the complaining association official, came over to tour the shop. No one made a fuss at all. One man actually laughed and said he didn't see anything wrong. Uncle Barry gave me a thumbs up on his way out, mission accomplished. But he was wrong. The association official was an attorney and he researched laws and city ordinances, looking for a way to shut me down. The property's zoning variance, which permitted retail in the building once zoned as a nursing home, provided that retail business at Chatham Center had to close early to accommodate neighbors. The official told Uncle Barry I needed to change my business hours to comply. Two days later I found out my shop was on the association meeting's agenda.

About forty people packed into the fire station on Mass Ave, leaving only a few chairs empty. Uncle Barry was there. The topic of my shop finally came up, described as an illegal adult business. The room got quiet.

A middle-aged guy in a flannel shirt and jeans stood up. "Seeing this shop in our neighborhood is disgusting! It should be shut down."

A smattering of claps followed. The daycare director commented on the sordid people who frequented the shop. "Think of the children," she said.

"I've been in the shop," a younger woman said. "She's not hurting anyone. Just leave her alone."

Another person who had been into the shop seconded the point. I sensed the room could be half in my favor.

Seizing the moment I stood up. "Most of my inventory cannot be legally defined as adult retail. I've studied the law and my inventory is tamer than what you see at Spencer's in the mall."

The lawyer spoke up again. "I move that we draft a letter to the city to ask for an investigation. Do I have a second?"

"Aye."

"Third?"

"Aye."

"A letter will be sent to the mayor's office."

Within a week two men rang my shop doorbell and gave me city zoning inspector business cards. I invited them in to look around. They started taking pictures.

"What is that?" one man asked.

"You're referring to a male chastity device," I said. "Those are used to prevent sex."

The other inspector asked how it worked.

"It locks on a man's genitalia and keeps him from having an erection."

"Sounds painful." They both laughed.

Two weeks later Uncle Barry told me the city's zoning report had concluded my shop did not meet the adult retail classification. The Reformatory could stay open but by then I was already in trouble. In the beginning business boomed but by fall the boutique was struggling. The shop wasn't doing the steady business required to succeed in the long run. During that time I took a few sessions, including the one with the undercover cop, to try and cover the cost of operations. Uncle Barry and I discussed my situation. I had tried and worked hard but I needed to close before I lost everything. I already knew that I had no other viable option. So I locked the door exactly one year after the Erotic Arts Ball. That date would be a reminder that life had both highs and lows, triumphs and defeats.

A month after I had closed the boutique for revenue reasons, Uncle Barry received an order as the building owner to shut down my business. The notice said retail could not be sold from the studio spaces. Apparently the retail zoning variance given to Chatham Center only applied to the gallery space and not the studios. The city split hairs and said nothing about the building's artists who retailed art from their spaces. I was singled out.

One cloudy day in late November, a Channel 6 news van pulled up in front of my house. Before I knew it, crime reporter Jack Rinehart and a cameraman were on my front porch for the second time.

"You can't come in! You aren't welcome here," I yelled through the glass.

Rinehart raised a sheet of paper so I could read it. I saw my name and the word defendant. He shouted that the city had filed a lawsuit against me.

My heart dropped. "Get off my property!" I shouted.

Then he told me the mayor was holding a press conference the next day, regarding my illegal businesses. Before I could say anything, a sheriff's car parked at the front curb and a deputy walked toward the house. Rinehart stepped aside as I opened the door. The deputy said he was serving me with a civil suit from the city. He gave me the document. Just like that the sheriff's deputy left and Rinehart, who just happened to arrive minutes before the law, packed his equipment in the Channel 6 van.

Skimming the city's complaint, I had no idea how to proceed, but I did understand I needed to be at the press conference. I got on the internet and started poking around for information. Finally a journalist friend got back to me and said the press conference would be the next morning at ten at the daycare center across the street from Chatham Center.

I called Derek and read part of it to him: ". . . the conduct of a business in which the defendant inflicts torture and/ or humiliation and/or performs specified sexual activities on patrons of her home occupation."

Derek told me to calm down and when he showed up that night, he insisted we go out as planned. He said it would be good for me to be with my friends at the Melody Inn. Every time I walked into the Mel, I felt like somebody.

"Miss Ann!" someone called as we entered the bar. "Heard on the radio tonight you're in trouble with the city."

"Thanks for chiming in, Danny," Derek said. "Is that your seventh or eighth whiskey?"

People were laughing which helped take the edge off, but I needed to get my ducks in a row for the press conference. I mean, the mayor of Indianapolis was addressing my business. Derek, Greg Brenner, Indy's premiere punk rock promoter, and I ordered drinks and began to talk shop. Derek suggested I just pay the fine and make it go away.

> " I understood I was a little off-kilter and stranger than the average person, but I was always taught that I was protected under the Constitution and had the right to be different as long as I didn't infringe upon the rights of others.

"I didn't do anything wrong! Why would I admit to committing a crime if I'm innocent?"

"This is bullshit!" Greg said, already a couple drinks ahead of us. "I'm going down there with you tomorrow, Miss Ann."

Greg and Derek traded stories and shots for a couple

more hours before I called it a night and went home. When I phoned Derek the next morning, he was too hungover to get out of bed. So I drove myself to what felt like my crucifixion, hoping to arrive under the radar. But the major news stations already had vans and camera crews there. About thirty people stood around the mayor's podium.

I was about to walk behind a group of women when one of them said, "I go to the church two doors down from her. It's horrible what she's doing in that house."

This again, I thought. I had to interrupt. "Excuse me, are you talking about the dominatrix?" I asked.

"Why yes, we are," she replied. "That's my parish and it's awful what she's doing to the neighborhood."

"I'm the dominatrix," I said. "Have I ever done anything to harm you?"

Then I saw Mayor Bart Peterson, six-five and handsome, walking down the sidewalk of the block where I'd operated the boutique. Peterson was a popular mayor who had done a lot for the city and I'd even voted for him twice. The day of the news conference, he as in the middle of his second term. Flanked by roughly twelve people, the mayor was being briefed before addressing the crowd.

"God, this is such bullshit," a voice said behind me.

Wearing sunglasses and his hair a mess, Greg stood behind me with a steaming cup of coffee. I was so relieved to see a friendly face.

"Good morning, sunshine," I said. "How do you feel this morning?"

Finally Peterson made his way to the podium which was outfitted with microphones. By that time about sixty people had shown up. Next to the mayor stood the pesky neighborhood association president, the daycare director and City Prosecutor Teri Kendrick. The production seemed too grand for a business that had recently closed for financial reasons. Peterson began by talking about preserving strict family values and enforcement of zoning codes. Then he turned to his administration's commitment to fight "these" kinds of businesses that were operating illegally.

I couldn't believe my ears. The city inspectors verified that my shop inventory did not legally qualify as adult. Two years earlier, a spokesperson for the Indianapolis Police Department went on record, saying my home-based business was legal and I had a right to operate it.

The speech concluded with Mayor Peterson asking for questions from the media.

I seethed with anger as a couple of reporters spoke up. Then I raised my hand. The same moment the mayor looked at me and pointed, a staffer spoke to him, no doubt informing him who I was.

"Do any of her businesses meet the legal definition of adult?" I asked.

Peterson stumbled and then said he was taking questions from the media.

"Do any of her businesses meet the legal definition of adult?" one of the reporters asked.

The question was deflected to Kendrick who said, no, the businesses in questions did not meet the legal definition of adult.

"Then what are we doing here?" another voice called out.

Kendrick explained that there were certain kinds of businesses that could be operated in the home, but the administration was taking the position that my business did not qualify. The media asked a few questions to pin down the definition of illegal adult business and Kendrick said again that nothing I was doing was criminal. She explained adult entertainment business as a technical term; however, in the dictionary the word adult meant adult in nature. Kink and merchandise for sexual and erotic torture were not what the Historic Preservation Commission imagined when it granted its zoning variance for gallery and studio space.

I was stunned. After the mayor stepped away from the dais, the attention shifted to me but I made my way over to Kendrick. "I'm hoping we can just talk about this and make it go away," I said to her.

Before Kendrick could respond, I was surrounded by reporters again.

"I do not want to have this conversation with the city attorney on film!" I said.

I had gotten so flustered, I couldn't even remember where my car was parked. I wandered through the parking lot with Greg until we ran into Paul Pogue and arranged to meet at the Old Point Tavern for an interview for *NUVO*.

I understood I was a little off-kilter and stranger than the average person, but I was always taught that I was protected under the Constitution and had the right to be different as long as I didn't infringe upon the rights of others. *NUVO*'s story took a few days to hit the newsstands. In the meantime, the only thing I could do was sit and wait for what came next.

Uncle Barry gave me an interesting tidbit. Before the press conference he'd called the mayor's office and told them my shop had already been closed for a full month, citing financial reasons for my decision. He said the mayor's office dismissed the information.

"Have you crunched the numbers involved in fighting this beast?" Derek asked that night. "You could pay the twenty-five hundred dollar fine. Or you could fight it and pay a lawyer two hundred fifty dollars an hour. After four hours, that's a thousand bucks. They charge you to talk on the phone, they charge you to see them in person."

My boyfriend thought I was in over my head. I started crying which, of course, led to hyperventilating. I couldn't control myself any longer.

"You could lose your house, Mely," Derek said. "The government has endless pockets of other people's money. It doesn't care if it ruins your life."

The press conference was incredibly traumatizing and I felt nothing inside except fear.

Yet I knew that even if it left me destitute, I had to walk into it. I remembered a premonition I had heard while meditating three years earlier–before Channel 6, my outing or the lawsuit had happened.

"One day you will have to face off with the government," the voice said.

"Oh, no not me!" I cried out in my mind.

"Oh yes, YOU! And when the time comes, you'll have every tool you need to prevail."

The answer I'd received in meditation comforted me and I had let it go until the day of the press conference. It seemed the time had finally come, but I had no idea how I would fight Goliath.

ChapterThirteen

I was broke, living off my credit card and selling shop assets on eBay, but I wouldn't let anyone see me ruffled in public. I wanted to look as unaffected as possible. Sub Justin hung around and went to fetish events with Derek and me. Justin didn't drink or date, lived with his aunt, drove a modest car and worked. To help me out, he drained his savings account to cover my mortgage and bills. Under the circumstances, I certainly couldn't have afforded to pay a lawyer.

Then Radford remembered Mark Small from Indiana University. He said he was an open-minded attorney who loved defending the Constitution. I needed a barrister with passion and personal drive to win. Radford thought Mark would welcome the media attention. Besides, Mark had also grown up in Palmerton. A close friend named Aaron set up an online legal defense fund for me and generously matched contributions dollar for dollar. I linked my PayPal account to the site for donations, switched my website content to my cause and linked to hundreds of sites. Cash came in from as far as California from kinksters who supported my fight with the city. When the fund grew to almost the same amount as Mark's fee, I saw it as the sign I needed to hire him.

Mark made fighting the lawsuit sound like an adventure. We were going to use the media to publicize my cause, not be used by the media. We were going to hold a press conference. I loved the gutsy idea of my own press conference but I was nervous. Mark told me not to worry because he would tell me what to say. I also asked Mark if he would go on the air with Abdul-Hakim Shabazz, a local radio personality, to do an interview about my case and take questions. We agreed I needed to stay visible in the media.

The next step was to put together a press release, announcing the press conference on the day we were going to file a response to the lawsuit. I had played enough chess to know that offense was how wars were won. I felt confident the city didn't foresee me dictating my own media coverage. I figured they expected me to shrink and pay their fine. But the mayor had put my lawsuit before the public and I was going to do everything I could to keep it there.

On January 20, Mark and I went down to Environmental Court on Virginia Avenue to file the response. As a part of our legal discovery, we submitted a request for production, specifically asking for any audio or video surveillance during the city's investigation. A couple of TV news reporters and Paul Pogue were waiting outside the building as we exited. Mark outlined the specifics of the interrogatories we'd filed and identified vagaries in the suit, calling for interpretations of the words masochism, erotic, and the phrase "sexually oriented torture, beating, or the infliction of pain."

"You can't limit someone's freedom through a statute or law that's excessively vague," Mark said in his statement. "They state that she inflicted torture and humiliation and engaged in sexual acts such as masochism and the erotic infliction of pain and humiliation. Those are not defined in the zoning ordinance. If you look at the definitions of torture that are defined in law, such as in the Geneva Conventions, I do not believe that any definition of torture by those treaties applies to my client. Zoning code delineates the categories of permissible businesses in residences. One of those is tutoring and education. My client teaches those who consult her for guidance and education."

Putting my face on television conjured a new set of fears in me. I needed a job but my name was all over the news and who would want to hire me after learning I was a dominatrix? I busied myself every day, applying for jobs and networking with old friends. My search turned up nothing. The anxiety of not knowing my future spiraled me into depression.

Sometime in February I thought about ending my life. Justin and Derek insisted I go see a therapist yet I didn't have money to pay one. I eventually found my way to a government sponsored counseling center.

Their professionals diagnosed me as depressed. I already knew I was depressed! The counselors referred me to a doctor who, after talking to me for about three minutes, wrote a prescription for an antidepressant. I'd had a bad experience once before with an antidepressant. My Yahoo! group was my own kind of therapy so I wrote about what was happening.

> I am not too proud or too weak to admit the truth of who I am. This can only make me stronger and serve to help others along the way. Hopefully, it will also serve to draw even more support for me, which I need very much. One thing that does not make me cry or feel weak is the legal fight. I am completely optimistic about prevailing and so is my attorney. I do not want anyone to ever think this court case has me down. Ironically, the court case is my one bright spot. I'm going to love challenging the lawsuit. And please know when I do it, I do it for all of us. This is bigger than just me.

One day I called Derek to see if he could come over but he said he would have to take a raincheck. He was busy practicing the snap of his dragon tail whip technique on water balloons in the bathroom. His goal was to perfectly strike without breaking the balloons. Meanwhile, he was also attempting mad scientist experiments in the kitchen with several chemicals he had purchased through a chemist supply website. He claimed the internet purchase could land him on an FBI watch list. Crazy, I knew. But I was no June Cleaver, either.

However, I could see our relationship was coming apart. He was a heavy drinker and liked the company of his friends who were younger than I was. He had serious health problems and I sometimes had to go over and play nurse or drive him to the emergency room. Then came February 22 and my birthday. Derek knew how important that day was to me but he forgot it. I was devastated. He tried to make amends by taking me to my favorite restaurant, but it was too late. I knew I couldn't count on him any longer. We stayed together because I didn't have the courage to break it off, but I realized I was on my own.

One day my phone rang with an opportunity to make some quick cash. An artist who lived in my neighborhood was aware of my predicament and offered me a job cleaning and organizing her house. When I arrived for duty the first day, I noticed amid the clutter in her kitchen an organized nook by the window. The space was an anomaly compared to the rest of the house.

"I've got to ask, Abigail. Why is this area perfect and everything else so cluttered?"

"It's my feng shui wealth area," she said. "I never have to worry about money."

Abigail explained the significance of each item. I was particularly interested in the large fishbowl with the beautiful long-tailed gold fish.

"Those are my water and fish elements," she said. "The glistening objects around the kitchen are my jewel elements. Having the perfect balance of all of these objects attracts wealth."

I'd heard of feng shui but didn't know anything about a wealth area. According to Abigail, it should be located in the back left part of the house. I went home, researched feng shui wealth on my computer and created my own wealth area. I must have intuitively understood how to do it because many of the items I had around my window were already perfectly placed.

A few days later, storm clouds gathered over Indianapolis. The sky spit golf ball-sized hail that struck the ground with the sound of leather on skin. After fifteen minutes, my lawn went from plush green to pure white. I went out to assess the damage and saw dents both on the roof of my car and my house. When all was said and done, I received a thirty-eight hundred dollar insurance check for my car but opted to pay bills instead. That same week, I accepted a sales job to help open the New York City market for a major dot com. Coincidence? I didn't think so.

The new job gave me a chance to see a proper therapist. I had a lot to say about what I was going through, the media attention, lawsuit, my job, my boyfriend, my bizarre out-of-the-box life. It took several sessions just to tell her how I became a dominatrix. Eventually, we arrived at my sexual abuse. I cried a lot during that session. My therapist was the first person to hear the specifics of what my half-brother had done to me and what I thought about as I was molested. She didn't say much at first except it was good to bring up the subject and she encouraged me to try to remember everything and get it all out. I told her I knew I couldn't change history and I felt that I was in charge of my life and the abuse didn't matter anymore.

> **As a domme I was in control. I administered the torture while consent made it moral. I was safe with a riding crop and a sub in chastity.**

"The child in you is still very hurt," she said.

My brain was still developing when the molestations occurred and the trauma had directed how my neural pathways formed. As an adult, my therapist told me, I needed to take care of that little girl and choose relationships that would protect her. Then she showed me the elephant in the room. How could I have not seen it before? Miss Ann was a character I'd created to reconcile the sexual abuse.

I was stunned. *That* was why I was so consumed with domination and submission in the beginning and why I dove so deeply into it so fast. D/s plugged directly into everything broken in me and was my path to repair it. As a domme I was in control. I administered the pain while consent made it moral. I was safe with a riding crop and a sub in chastity. No one could violate me if I was in charge.

The therapist told me to start telling my close friends about the abuse. She warned it would cause some who knew my abuser to distance themselves, but she said I was better off having a smaller inner circle of friends anyway. Talking about it would lead to healing. I didn't want to talk about it but knew I had to.

I was still Miss Ann even though I was no longer working as a dominatrix and I stuck with Derek. Something about dating a dom was intoxicating. Maybe it was his power or his confidence and devil-may-care attitude. Maybe it was because Derek was so wild and outrageous that I couldn't have enough. Something about walking into those fetish events with Derek invigorated me. I was Miss Ann, the dominatrix all over the news, standing tall in the face of adversity with her elegant boyfriend. I felt like a star. We even had our own little entourage to follow us around. Sub Justin became Maid Gigi in a black satin maid's uniform, a frilly petticoat, a latex mask and wig.

Despite the dissolving of InKink, the monthly slave auctions continued to be the only fetish event in Indianapolis. This created an awkward setting as my old nemeses Liza, Sparrow and the Fluttering Menace were always in attendance. I had stopped speaking to them after refunding memberships but was civil in public. Other kinksters were finished with them, too, having grown tired of their games. But the trio never went away. The Menace still emceed the auctions.

At the first auction following the press conference, I purchased multiple slaves and had them perform for me and the crowd. The Menace didn't share my sense of humor. She declared a new rule–buyers could only purchase one sub. I broke the rule by creating a loophole, giving my friends money to purchase slaves for me. Once owned, they were free to give away their purchases if they chose. Eventually a new event producer, Stevie, took over the fetish party. Derek and I wanted to raise the ante for subs. I said twenty dollars, he said fifty. We met with the club owner and agreed a charity event and new auctioneer would increase the crowd and elevate the status of the event. I handled the process of recruiting the slaves from the crowd by approaching the most colorful submissives who would bring the most money.

Our first event was called Back To School. We hoped to fill the crowd with dozens of naughty school girls. I dressed as the lunch lady and carried a giant rubber spatula for spanking. Stevie came as a janitor with a mop bucket on wheels and Derek dressed as a mad science teacher with goggles and a long white lab coat. I was in charge of selecting the charity for the evening. A former teacher of mine had started an orphanage and school in Kenya for children whose parents had died of AIDS. I called my teacher to explain our plan. She had no qualms or judgments whatsoever about our kinky proclivities. The school needed a sponsor to pay for a sewing teacher.

"I have for sale lot number twelve, also known as Vanessa," Derek called out.

The crowd laughed as the sexy brunette in a black party dress spun around for the crowd.

"We'll start the bidding at twenty dollars."

A football coach immediately raised his hand and blew his whistle.

"Do we have thirty?"

"Thirty!" a goth chick screamed.

The back and forth ended at eighty dollars. That was the highest amount a sub had ever brought. By the end of the auction, we had raised eight hundred dollars for the school. The next morning my teacher said there would also be enough extra money to buy fabric for new school uniforms. After that, the auctions continued to be a great success. The biggest one raised over three thousand dollars for Stevie's favorite charity, the AIDS walk. The event transitioned from just a party to an evening with a purpose.

While I endured the hazards of the underground kink scene, learning the politics of a city the size of Indianapolis was just as complicated. Getting to know the real nature of all the players could take a long time. I had to put in the hours if I was going to understand the intricacies of City Hall. The city government had tried to put me in bondage but powerful men didn't intimidate me. I had seen them in lingerie and a chastity device, groveling. They had paid money to kiss my feet and relinquish control. It was easy for me to see the mayor and other public servants as submissive to the electorate. A power exchange needed to take place.

Indy had a variety of political blogs published by citizen journalists, lawyers and activists. Blogs were still relatively new in Indy social media but they were rapidly multiplying and gaining attention. The writers often published penetrating stories based on news articles and received tips from government insiders. By the summer of 2006, I was dedicating ten hours or more a week, studying blogs and reading local political news.

Sometimes the mainstream media hijacked stories that had been leaked online, not giving credit to bloggers like Gary Welsh, a former lobbyist and local attorney who wrote Advance Indiana. Another blog I followed was Indy Undercover, supposedly written by a police officer who used the moniker Joe Friday, updating his post several times a day. Indy Undercover was popular among cops because their concerns were given a voice. Blogs sometimes floated questions about city officials along with rumors.

That summer Mark scheduled a deposition of the vice cop and zoning officials. Derek tagged along dressed like Wall Street and Mark wore a seer-sucker suit and baseball cap. The first thing he did was crack some baseball jokes. He must have been trying to throw off the opposition. Former vice cop Don was sworn in first. He said he had worked for the police department for over thirty years and retired shortly after his session with me.

> **Q:** As a result of your investigation of Miss Ann, did you find that she was engaged in any criminal conduct?
>
> **A:** No. Not to the point where I could make an arrest, no.

Don then said he had worn a whisper device and that another detective recorded our conversation in a van across the street.

> **Q:** Miss Ann showed you two types of lingerie and told you to pick the one you wanted to wear. Is that accurate?
>
> **A:** Yes.
>
> **Q:** What were the two pieces of lingerie like?
>
> **A:** A one-piece and a two-piece. The one-piece had a thong type bottom and the two-piece looked easier to get on.
>
> **Q:** I'm sorry?
>
> **A:** The two-piece looked easier to get on, so I chose the two-piece.
>
> **Q:** I didn't want to assume it had something to do with the color or style.

We laughed. Mark's questions got more serious when he asked Don about my refusal to have sex with him.

> **A:** Reflecting back on my experience, prostitutes never admit to being prostitutes. And because she said she wasn't a prostitute didn't mean to me that she wasn't.

Despite my anger at the time, I began to realize that Don was just doing his job. Even so, it was hard to reconcile the feeling of being violated by the city when one of its employees entered my home to ask for sex several times.

A month after that deposition, City Attorney Teri Kendrick deposed me in return. She asked me how I taught D/s.

> **A:** It's a vast subject, but primarily I teach that to serve another human being is our highest good.
>
> **Q:** How is that?
>
> **A:** By inspiring servitude.
>
> **Q:** How do you do that?
>
> **A:** I give people permission to be who they are inside as an individual. I don't judge them but instead give them a platform for self-expression. It frees them.
>
> **Q:** And while you're freeing them, what is physically happening?
>
> **A:** It's not necessarily a physical experience. It's a spiritual, it's a psychological, it's a mental experience. The physical is really not where my interest lies.
>
> **Q:** Well, it's where my interest lies, Miss Ann, and I'd appreciate it if you'd answer the question. Physically what do you do to provide this inspiration that you have described?
>
> **A:** I don't use physical contact to inspire.

The rest of the deposition outlined the use of each one of my implements. Kendrick also inquired about how I registered my occupation for tax purposes, to which I agreed I was a self-employed entertainer.

"Julie was saying something I'd been feeling but wasn't ready to admit. She helped me see the light. Right then and there, I killed off Miss Ann.

The legal process dragged on at a snail's pace while the slave auctions continued to flourish. The crack in the foundation I had built with Derek was widening. He was thirty-something, dating a woman in her forties. He always wanted to hang out with a younger crowd. I loved Derek and secretly wanted to just settle down but we really didn't even like doing the same things. Car racing was the antithesis of going to an art gallery. One night he ended the relationship and of course, I was crushed. I later told my friend Neal that I'd made a fundamental discovery about the relationship. I was pretty sure Derek never loved Mely. He loved Miss Ann.

I began to feel that I wasn't as good as my persona. Miss Ann was fabulous. Mely was ordinary. But the truth was, Miss Ann was never real, she was an invention. When people found out I was a dominatrix, they usually didn't understand that my vulnerable side still existed behind the mask. I decided I should go to the next fetish event and made myself show up. Because Derek and I ran the slave auctions and had split up, the energy at the party felt hollow. I didn't belong there anymore but had nowhere else to go.

A popular domme came to the party that night. Over the past year we had become good friends in spite of the differences between us. Julie identified herself with a dark aura in the shadows and saw me as always carrying the light. We loved discussing our contrasting personas. That night she hosted a midnight party when the club closed so I drove to her place. Derek was there but he avoided me and I didn't have much to say.

"Your expression hasn't changed all night," Julie said. "What is it?"

"I guess I'm just depressed about Derek."

"No, it's bigger than that," she said.

"What are you getting at?"

"You don't belong here," Julie told me.

I must have known she was right. Tears started streaming down my face.

"Look around, Miss Ann. You're different. Everything here . . . It's dark. You're aware of it. This world isn't for you."

Julie was saying something I'd been feeling but wasn't ready to admit.

"I'm not going to let you stay," she said. "And you have to leave now."

I didn't really want to leave her inviting home, but it had been a long time since anyone had understood exactly what I needed. In a sense Julie helped me see the light.

Right then and there, I killed off Miss Ann.

My friends from the kink scene didn't call or try to contact me. Niles and Neal were in my corner but otherwise any communication I had with that crowd evaporated. I didn't deal with the change in my life very well. I had gained about twenty-five pounds since Derek and I split and a rash had formed on my chest. I was uninspired to cook food at home and lived on carryout and watched movies in the dark. Work, eat, veg out, sleep. Over and over. I hadn't even made friends at work. People were slow to warm up to a dominatrix.

The first friend I made at my new job was Jules Bush. She was gay and understood societal judgment. When people made incorrect assumptions, she stood up for me and educated them. We went to lunch together once a week and she helped me feel connected.

Once a month Abdul hosted a happy hour at Nicky Blaine's martini bar for his followers. When I was ready, I decided to get out of the house and do a little networking. Neal went with me. As fortune would have it, I ran into an old acquaintance and we got caught up on each other's lives. Then the subject switched to politics, more specifically the Fair Tax. I had learned about the Fair Tax through the

Neal Boortz Show and was glad to hear someone else waxing on about its benefits. The Fair Tax was a plan to replace income tax with a consumption tax and abolish the IRS. My friend was a business partner of Sean O'Neal, a co-director for Fair Tax in the state. Apparently Sean needed a volunteer to run projects and get things done, specifically help with creating awareness in Indiana that a viable plan existed to eliminate the IRS.

Before I knew it, I was meeting with Sean over drinks to discuss Fair Tax in more depth. Part of my volunteering would include calling people who had signed up for more information. Since I had a day job, I started spending evenings on the phone, encouraging my fellow citizens to call their congressman in support of the Fair Tax plan. Sean had a list of thousands of people for me to contact. Conversations took time. I also set up gatherings at the Legal Beagle, a downtown watering hole frequented by lawyer types. I emailed invites to friends and a few people showed up but I wasn't getting enough traction to do much of anything useful. I needed the media.

ChapterFourteen

In 2007, a property tax nightmare was looming quietly in the background of Indiana politics. Three years earlier Indiana voters had repealed the business inventory tax to take effect in 2007, which would save small business owners about four hundred million dollars per year. Local governments relied upon receiving this tax revenue every spring, and with the business inventory tax cancelled, counties were running out of money. The legislature decided the deficit should be recouped through property taxes, calling for new property assessments to be carried out by each county individually.

After reassessments were underway, political blogs squawked that many counties, including Indianapolis' Marion County, couldn't properly handle the reassessments. Rumors swirled that assessors were blindly estimating the value of homes, calculating taxes that had no rhyme or reason. By June 2007, the new assessments were finally completed and ready for view. Bloggers linked Marion County's website to show property tax history and appraised values for every address. I plugged in several addresses around my neighborhood and found the tax increases downright frightening. Most bills tripled, some quadrupled or more. My taxes went from eleven hundred dollars per year to nearly four thousand dollars.

On top of that, the inconsistency of appraisals was baffling. Similar properties had drastically different values with discrepancies as high as one hundred thousand dollars. Some homes were assessed at values higher than the properties were worth. Simultaneously, the housing bubble had burst and real estate values were tumbling nationwide. What about the older folks in my neighborhood who lived on fixed incomes? Some had lived in their homes for decades and would be forced to move.

Blogs seemed to be the only place where the gravity of the situation was being spelled out. The local news ran stories as if light rain was on the way when in truth a hurricane was gathering. This was the perfect storm to blow the Fair Tax into our local media, which had been my task as a volunteer for the past six months. Here was an example of unfair taxation dropped right into my own backyard and people were going to want to talk about it. I had access to a team of leaders, Fair Tax directors and simpatico key players within the Libertarian Party. Turbulence about property taxes gave me an opening to talk up the Fair Tax plan.

As a dominatrix I was keenly aware that people often didn't move unless they felt pain, and excruciating pain was about to hit their wallets. I needed to personally connect with as many neighbors as possible before their bills arrived on July third. My plan was to form a Fair Tax volunteer posse to bike around my neighborhood, warn homeowners and tell them where to rally to hear a solution. I asked a few friends who also supported the Fair Tax plan if they'd join me in spreading the word about a Fourth of July rally in front of the governor's mansion, Indiana's symbolic home located in the middle of my neighborhood, Meridian-Kessler. If I could persuade my neighbors to take to the streets within hours of receiving their bills, TV and print media would likely show up. An affluent homeowners' protest was newsworthy.

The Saturday night before I was to lead my bicycle posse around the community, I stayed up late making Hoosiers for Fair Taxation flyers. But by ten the next morning, none of my volunteers had shown up. I didn't want to ride by myself but I knew I had to muster the courage. I had an innate sense that it was one of those pivotal moments in life but no idea where it would lead. Instead of blowing off the plan, I decided to go it alone. If I failed, I might look like a fool for trying, but it seemed critical to do what I could. Besides, I would feel like a failure inside if I quit.

The weather was perfect so I rode around and talked to people working in their yards. If they hadn't seen their tax bills online, I warned them they weren't going to be happy when the bills arrived in their mailboxes. Then I gave them a Fair Tax brochure on which I'd put my homemade printed sticker labels announcing the Fourth of July rally.

I ended the day at a friend's house in Butler-Tarkington, a nearby neighborhood named after Butler University and Indiana writer Booth Tarkington. She was excited to hear that people were organizing to fight the tax increases and, as a single homeowner, was worried about her bill. While at her house I got on the phone and called Abdul to let him know what I'd done. He agreed to announce the rally on his radio program. It felt good knowing I already had a little bit of media in the tank.

The next day a local politician, Andy Horning, called to say he would help me handle the rally. Co-Fair Tax Director, Sean Shepard said he would also be on hand at the governor's mansion on Meridian Street.

I remembered years earlier riding along Meridian with my mom. I pressed my face to the car window as we passed the majestic old mansions built by post-industrial revolution wealth. Mom said not only could we never afford one of those castles, we couldn't even pay the property taxes.

"What are property taxes?" I asked.

"That's what the government charges you to live in your house."

Mom's perspective seemed weirdly prophetic.

Knowing little about government and actual policy, I was clueless about what to say to protesters when they gathered so it was a relief to hear Andy would bring the boys who knew policy to run the show. I'd always had a knack for getting people to move and gather at parties, fetish events, the Erotic Arts Ball—a political demonstration would be no different. Everyone had a job and mine happened to be public relations and marketing.

> Maybe I'd found a way to get even. Now only four months before the general election in November, I thought enough public angst might exist to overthrow the mayor.

The day of the rally I dressed in blue with a polka-dot scarf on my head and arrived on my bike, carrying my beloved Indiana state flag. About a hundred people and all the news stations were waiting for the rally to start. Andy started speaking over the PA about the necessity of taxes being transparent and that transparent taxes were based on consumption, which gave citizens a choice.

"We've let government get out of our hands," Andy said.

The crowd grew and protesters spilled into Meridian Street, causing a traffic back-up.

"I didn't expect this to stop traffic," Andy said. "It's great you guys have the will to do something!"

Angry, motivated people were ready to march. Before long an estimated five hundred had shown up for the tax rally at the governor's mansion obviously because the issue was personal and affected their finances. I was learning it wasn't hard to get people moving if the right cause came along.

Then I had a devious thought. With property taxes skyrocketing, Peterson had announced he was raising the County Option Income Tax (COIT). The COIT hike alone wouldn't turn people against Peterson, but the thought of two new tax increases might be enough to direct some of the public outrage his way. Peterson had nothing to do with state property taxes, I knew that, but I held a lot of resentment for the way City Hall had come after me. The vice cop, media showing up at my house, a press conference with the mayor denouncing my businesses and then the lawsuit. Who wouldn't be angry? Maybe I'd found a way to even the score. Now only four months before the general election in November and nineteen months after the mayor's action against me, I thought enough public angst might exist to overthrow him.

"We need a tea party!" someone shouted.

"And if they don't listen to us, step three is Boston Tea Party time," Andy said.

If the people wanted a party, I could give it to them. I just had to figure out where, when and how! What seemed like a never-ending line of citizens formed behind Andy to vent over the PA system. As the rally wore on, the crowd continued to grow. The police set up roadblocks on Meridian Street, our city's main artery, and rerouted traffic headed downtown for the Fourth of July festivities.

One sign read, "Nice Stadium. Can we live there?" This referred to Lucas Oil Stadium, another taxpayer nightmare. The most effective placards at the rally might have been the most simple. At least twenty people toted store-bought "For Sale By Owner" signs. Since many protesters had the same idea, I decided to specialize the message for our cause. "For Sale By Owner Due To Unfair Taxation" were words that would make the news. After the rally I found a company to manufacture the signs in bulk and Sullivan Hardware, our popular neighborhood home and garden retailer, offered to fund their production and sell them at cost. The next thing I knew, hundreds of homes in the Meridian-Kessler community had planted the red and white signs in their yards. It was especially exciting to see the signs in the manicured front lawns of countless mansions along the city's historic Meridian corridor. The signs made the news overnight.

Within a week Governor Daniels created campaign-funded literature to communicate with homeowners. The cover of his flyer was a color picture of my sign. It addressed the property tax crisis, blaming local government debt, poor assessing and overspending at the county level. We had the attention of the most powerful man in the state.

I knew if five hundred people showed up at a rally and protesters were calling for tea parties, this thing was only going to get bigger. I needed to create a blog where we could link our media coverage and announcements of future protests, meetings and other events. The day after the first rally on July 5, my Hoosiers for Fair Taxation blog went live.

My first post linked all the rally coverage. I used an email list collected at the governor's mansion to announce the blog, encouraging everyone to share the site with interested parties. Moving forward, Hoosiers for Fair Taxation became a central forum for updates on all matters related to the property tax crisis. In time, it also reported on other government matters, both local and federal. The first rally was covered by all the local news stations and the *Indianapolis Star*. Hundreds of people visited my website daily. I found myself at work, fielding calls from the media all day and spending my evenings on the phone with other activists.

At the first rally Mike Rowe, a local realtor, announced Black Sunday at Monument Circle on July 15. I wasn't sure what exactly Black Sunday meant at the time. The next day Mike contacted me to help coordinate the communication for his event. He also alerted the media and soon Black Sunday was a topic on local airwaves, the blogs and the newspaper. Supporters were to wear black to show unity, carry signs and march around Monument Circle. Black Sunday promised to be more organized and much larger than our first rally.

Meanwhile, Sean Shepard and Andy Horning needed my help again. They wanted 40 put on an educational forum called Fair Tax 101 at Talbot Street, a gay bar and nightclub. Talbot Street donated space for the meeting. My job was to help put fannies in the seats, notify the media and greet people.

On July 9, about two hundred squeezed into the room to listen to Andy and Sean. Six months earlier, I had barely gotten twelve people to meet at the Legal Beagle but that night I had a packed house. After the forum, several gathered at the Living Room Lounge on Pennsylvania Street to continue talking. The forum was covered on the eleven o'clock news. "The people have been calling for a tea party, Sean," I said. "I don't know exactly how to throw one."

"We could make a giant tea bag and have people put their assessments in it," Sean said.

"I can get a tea bag made!" I said. "How about if we dunk the tea bag into the canal?"

I put up a post for a Betsy Ross volunteer to stitch yards of white fabric I had on hand into a giant tea bag. A woman called the next day and a week later, I returned to her house to pick up the finished product. It far exceeded my expectations with the words "Hoosiers for Fair Taxation" appliqued in gold and blue on it along with an Indiana state flag. The top was made to accommodate a drawstring rope for dunking the tea bag from a bridge into the Central Canal.

Then the Howey Political Report published an article detailing a statement issued by Governor Daniels. As it turned out, the governor had been on a family vacation when the tax bills came out. He said the hikes were the fault of state government and he would do everything in his power to fix the crisis. He declared tax payments were suspended until further notice. In spite of this gesture, we had to stay on task to ensure solutions and permanent change. Protesting gave people an outlet for their anger and showed the government we weren't backing off. We wanted to hold the government accountable.

On Black Sunday I parked and carried my Indiana flag toward the Circle, running into Mark Rutherford, former chair of the state Libertarian Party. Mark gave me the nod for carrying the Indiana flag instead of the national flag. About fifty folks had already assembled with signs, but before long, the crowd swelled to a thousand people in black, marching. Dozens carried "For Sale By Owner Due to Unfair Taxation" signs, "Say No to King George," "Extortion!" and "Bart Lies." For two hours the crowd swirled around Monument Circle downtown. Eventually we marched two blocks up Market Street to the state house. There we stood on the north steps as individual protesters took turns venting into a bullhorn. For a solid hour I heard the voices of fellow citizens, united in the cause of holding government accountable. People were taking responsibility and owning their dominance.

About a week after the rally, I was invited to a party at an activist's house. We imbibed and talked about the fair tax tea party scheduled at the end of the month. I caught the eye of a cute younger guy with mussed-up locks who seemed eager to talk with me. He introduced himself as Max. We chatted and the story of my career as a dominatrix came out.

"I think I might need you to keep me in line," Max said. "Could you do that for me?"

I had no interest in taking on a sub but was still enjoying the attention of such a good-looking guy. And he was a great listener so I didn't shoo him away. Instead, I ranted to him about how the government was supposed to be submissive to the people and how citizens weren't owning their role as dominants. Before leaving, I relented and gave Max my phone number. He started calling me the next morning.

Max, I soon learned, was a compassionate, capable and engaging young man. With the tea party looming, I thought of a role for him to play. A group of elderly women were going to dunk the tea bag full of assessments into the canal. Neighborhood seniors were most vested and had the most to lose from a property tax hike. Because the tea party would surely be on the news, I thought demonstrating their vulnerability would elicit sympathy for our cause. We needed an able-bodied man to assist the ladies and it didn't hurt that Max had a great face for television, either.

"You're going to be the face of a revolution," I told him.

Kim King, a reporter from Fox 59, called to arrange a personal interview with me at my house. She wanted to know why we were holding the tea party, who planned to attend and what we expected from politicians. After the interview concluded, we drove two miles up the street to the corner of Central Avenue and Westfield Boulevard. There she did a remote broadcast, showing where the tea bag would be ceremoniously lowered from the bridge into the canal.

July 28, 2007, was a typical humid day in Indiana. I put on my new custom-made T-shirt which read, "We The People expect all property tax to be repealed and replaced with a more fair form of taxation." The day before, I'd stuffed my fridge with soft drinks, frozen pizzas and beer for an activist meeting after the demonstration. Max came by and we gathered together the tea bag with its fifty-foot drawstring rope and drove to the canal. Milling around with the giant tea bag open, Max instructed people to toss their assessments inside. Some of the crowd came in costumes as Native Americans, the Statue of Liberty and colonial patriots. One sign held by a young girl read, "Taxes or Tuition, My Parents Can't Do Both."

Only a couple of elected politicians showed their faces. David Orentlicher, a three-term democratic state legislator, was brave enough to take a smattering of verbal tomatoes and offered his statist rhetoric toward our concerns. In the face of a riled up constituency, he said he was committed to being part of the solution, despite his stance on keeping property taxes in place. His presence proved that at least he cared.

Mayoral candidate Greg Ballard was there, too, shaking hands. Even though he was inexperienced, the Republicans had given him the nomination. With the election being three months out, I'd heard he had only fifty thousand dollars in his campaign chest compared to Peterson's $2.5 million. A retired marine corps lieutenant colonel, Ballard was the underdog but he supported property tax repeal and had said so publicly more than once. So he was our man.

The rally started like all the others. News cameras were present and speakers took to the microphone to lead the charge. Rev. Mmoja Ajabu, an ex-Black Panther who converted to Christianity and was Minister of Social Concerns at an African-American mega-church, preached about why taxing the land was wrong from a biblical perspective.

With the crowd fired up, Sean Shepard took the microphone and delivered the last speech, summarizing the views of the crowd that day. He ended by saying, "We further state, without dissent among the governed that no person should ever, ever fail to be secure in their home or dwelling because the state has demanded a never-ending tax or duty upon the mere ownership of it."

He paused a moment before giving the final order.

"Why don't we show the government what we think of our tax assessments!" he shouted.

Hundreds of onlookers and media focused their attention on the bridge while Max and the senior ladies lowered the tea bag into the canal. Flags waved in the background and the crowd roared as the tea bag steeped for a few minutes, saturating our assessments.

> I realized the whole movement–everything from my bike ride to the tea party and this rally– was grassroots. Ballard's campaign didn't have a hand in any of it. The people of Indianapolis made it all happen.

After the ceremonial dunking, I spotted an activist called the Scotsman and Dave Bond, founder of S.T.O.P.Indiana. "Pizza and beer at my house," I told them. "I can feed everyone who wants to get on board."

Shepard and Horning were coming and Ajabu had confirmed. I also recruited Pastor Joe Quintana, a former NYC cop who ministered to an inner city church on the near south side. I chatted up blogger IndyErnie of the

"Bart Lies" camp and Flipper, a retired firefighter who was Ballard's campaign driver.

When we got to my house, Pastor Joe noticed a riding crop on my mantle and wondered out loud if I was an equestrian. Someone informed him otherwise.

"Quite a colorful collection of people, isn't it!" the Scotsman said.

About twenty-five people had showed up. We were Republican, Democrat, Libertarian and Independent with different ethnicities, education, employment, personal beliefs, religions, social and economic backgrounds. Calling our crowd diverse was an understatement. We had to stay nonpartisan because we were against unfair property taxes, not any one party's agenda. We all felt the government was getting too big, was trampling over its citizens, and we had united to incite change.

Chris Spangle, who went on to become the Indiana Libertarian Party state director, later called us the The Justice League. That made me feel like a super heroine.

When the subject of property taxes came up, as it often did over the next few months, television news rolled our tea party footage. I got some measure of the impact from the number of calls Max received from buddies wondering how he'd managed to put himself in the spotlight.

A few days after the tea party, a man named Paul spoke to me in a fast food joint near City Hall and asked if I'd seen him in his pirate costume at the protest. I did remember him. He said the pirate outfit was all he had at the time but asked if he could wear a colonial costume to the rest of the rallies.

"Are you kidding?" I said. "That would be brilliant!"

Days later he called to say he had his costume and was ready to report for duty. With a tri-corner hat, knickers, stockings, buckled shoes and a long wool coat, Patriot Paul looked the part of an authentic colonial. He became a symbol for the cause in the upcoming events and time and time again, the media filmed and photographed him. Paul became a local celebrity of sorts after being pictured in his patriot outfit so many times.

That summer after twenty months and without any fanfare, the city finally offered to dismiss my lawsuit. Mark called to tell me he had the paperwork ready for my signature. We had expected a dismissal all along and Mark had taken care of everything, so the long drawn-out conclusion turned out to be anticlimactic. By then, I was obsessed with the tax issue.

One steamy afternoon Max and I rushed to a city council meeting. We'd received word that Peterson's camp had sent out text messages for city employees to pack the seats. Word to arrive early spread like wildfire through our ranks. Max and I pushed through the revolving doors of City Hall, passed through the metal detectors and made our way upstairs.

About a hundred people were already packed like sardines on the mezzanine level. I noticed the council chamber doors were shut. What was happening? Anyone was allowed to attend city council meetings. Something was fishy. It took me a second then I spotted the guards standing outside each set of doors to the auditorium. Max and I headed for an entrance.

"Someone locked us out," an activist said. "There's no point in trying."

I jiggled the door handles. "Why can't we get in?" I asked a guard.

He shrugged. "I was told not to let anyone in. I don't even have the key."

It was ninety-eight degrees outside and the air conditioning couldn't keep up with the heat and the crowd. Out of the corner of my eye, I noticed a few people going in through the west entrance so I went over to that guard and demanded he let us in. He stared blankly at me and said I was out of luck.

"What makes those people so special?" I asked.

He hesitated for a few seconds. "I was instructed to only allow city employees into the chamber," he said.

"Excuse me everyone," I said loudly to make my voice fill the area outside the chamber. I'd made my way to the center of the crowd. "May I have your attention? It appears only Peterson's comrades are being allowed inside. I don't know about you, but if my employees locked me out of my building, they'd be fired immediately." My words seemed to further rile the already angry citizens.

Shortly after my announcement, the guards caved and let us go in. Most of the seats were taken by then, but that didn't matter. We'd line the aisles if we had to. After the meeting, I told an *Indianapolis Star* political reporter what had happened and drilled into his head that we were blatantly denied entrance and our story must be told. I had to do everything in my power to make sure the public knew the truth the next day. Luckily for us, pictures of packed-in citizens hit televisions later that night. Indy's media did the right thing by including our lockout drama in their segments on the 2008 city budget.

Max was still hanging around. I thought of him as a politically active kid in his twenties, trying to get more involved. Despite being smart and quirky, he was, quite frankly, annoying at first. But after a while I started to feel a strange mental connection and it wasn't long before I realized I was into this guy. What was I getting myself into? A woman in her forties falling for a younger man in his twenties? I needed a reality check! I asked some girlfriends at work what they thought.

"Honey," one said. "Absolutely go for it. You might not have another chance at something like this. It's not like you have children or anything stopping you. Why not?"

That day I embraced dating a twenty-five-year-old and bit the bullet on the perception of becoming a cougar. I figured the enjoyment of being with Max would far outweigh the awkwardness. Turned out I was right–we sizzled together. We were both into metaphysics and shared an interest in both the physical and the spiritual world. Max liked everything about me–the domme, the political activist, the new age believer, the vulnerable person. He went with me to all my meetings and after a short time, he made a bold move.

"You're an activist and putting yourself out there," Max said one day. "And here you are living in this house by yourself with no one to protect you. I'm moving in."

Fully living the life of a political activist, I did little else. Max loved being in the center of ground zero for the property tax revolt. When I wasn't in meetings, at rallies, forums or on the phone with other activists, Max and I were together at home.

In late September, Tony Rehagen from *Indianapolis Monthly* phoned me at my office and said he wanted to do a piece on my metamorphosis from dominatrix to tax activist. He proposed to shadow me all the way up to the election in November. Wow! Since he was friends with a journalist I knew, I was inclined to trust him. I just had to make sure it was cool with hosts of the activist meetings to bring media along.

All the while we kept up our protest antics. One afternoon Reverend Ajabu helped make smashing theater out of a City Hall protest. It was brilliant! Within minutes of arriving, he had organized the crowd of a hundred in front of the building. The sign-toting protesters kept their feet moving to avoid trouble but once inside the meeting, Ajabu had choreographed hecklers to yell at city councilors. He assigned twenty recruits a number and after the meeting started, he signaled them one-by-one to stand up and shout. The discussion that evening was about COIT.

"How dare you raise our income tax when we have property tax bills we can't pay!" number one screamed.

A Marion County deputy immediately took the heckler by the elbow and escorted him from the auditorium. After about a minute, order was restored. Next, Ajabu held up two fingers.

"You spend spend spend! Where's the accountability?" number two shouted.

The disruptions went on until all twenty had been escorted from the meeting. I never in a million years would have expected a former Black Panther to command soldiers from Meridian-Kessler in a protest against the government. It was civil disobedience at its finest.

The Scotsman was a genius when it came to staging a spectacle. He served on the front line at every protest and contributed the most creative ideas. He was adamant we fulfill one particular fantasy that was not-for-the-casual-sign-toter. He wanted to get up early and picket outside the mayor's northside home–Breakfast at Bart's. As soon as the idea was on the table, I knew it had to happen. We all agreed to keep it under wraps until we had the right reason to bring his brainchild to life.

A Peterson campaign commercial in August gave us the motivation we needed to go ahead. Protesting at the mayor's residence was a sensitive operation and some of our regulars would be too timid to attend. I also knew ten people at a protest was a non-story. The problem was how to engage news stations with only a handful of protesters.

The media loved two things, controversy and mystery, so I sent a press release promising a secret protest the next Sunday morning, instructing media to telephone me early for the location. They'd have to hustle to get there by eight. Ten of us with signs met at Joe's Crab Shack and then caravanned to Bart's house Sunday morning. Right after we got there, a print journalist and three TV camera crews showed up.

We shouted for the mayor to come out but no one appeared until security materialized and told us not to step on the property. We stayed in the street and rallied for about an hour and half but never saw the mayor. We couldn't tell if he was home or not. I thought it would have been be a great PR move for his campaign if he had walked out the front door in his robe with a coffee pot in hand and invited us in for a Danish and a morning chat. That's what I would have done. He might have won the election if he had. The next day, the Indianapolis Star ran a feature spread in its political section about Breakfast at Bart's with color photos and quotes from us.

During October, we immortalized Peterson and City Council President Monroe Gray in a Halloween Yard of Shame. The Mayor was Count Bart-u-la, a huge photoshopped vampire with the caption, "I'll suck you dry." Monroe Gray was the "Unfriendly Ghost Employee," referring to a blog rumor about his salary from the fire department where he allegedly never showed up to work. We caricatured Councilwoman JoAnne Sanders with a witch hat and the caption, "I'll tax you and your little dog, too!" Councilman Paul Bateman who later pled guilty to thirteen counts of money laundering, was called simply "Master Bateman."

One afternoon, Tony Rehagen, *The Indianapolis Monthly* journalist, Max and I were hanging out at the house. I heard about a pro-Ballard parade on Broad Ripple Avenue and thought it would be good for Rahagen to document the ever increasing support for Indy's underdog candidate. We hopped in the car and went to join the parade of about seventy-five activists holding signs and wearing Ballard T-shirts. Cars honked and drivers yelled at us out their windows. Side-by-side with fellow voters, something struck a chord that day. I realized the whole movement–everything from my bike ride to the tea party and this rally–was grassroots. Ballard's campaign didn't have a hand in any of it. The people of Indianapolis made this all happen and I couldn't help but feel proud of my role in it.

We weren't the only group campaigning against Peterson. Other citizen groups had organized to protest the property tax issue. When Rehagen began shadowing me, I started to believe we could win. Indy's flagship magazine paying a journalist to cover me for a whole month meant the activists were on somebody's radar. According to a mid-September poll from WISH-TV, Peterson had led Ballard fifty-two percent to thirty-eight percent but by late October, about a week before the election, the mayor's lead had sunk to forty-three percent to thirty-nine percent. Anything seemed possible.

As all our energy and action were about to become part of the final equation, I felt a strong need to nourish the spirit of our efforts with a symbolic gesture. Since childhood, I'd had an intense fascination with rocks and learned through my new age reading that each type of stone had a unique energy that could be directed and used. I decided to get some crystals for a ceremony I wanted to perform and went to my favorite rock and crystal emporium, All My Relations. The shop's name reflected the owner's philosophy about the inter-relatedness and connection of all souls through spirit. I introduced myself to Heather and found out she was also a sergeant in the police department.

"No kidding! I can't believe you're a cop and you own a crystal shop," I said.

"You'd be surprised how many police officers are open-minded about this."

"Really?"

"There's a mass awakening about spirituality and holistic healing, even among cops."

I asked her if she read the IndyUndercover blog and she said she was very familiar with it.

"So are you supporting Ballard or Peterson?"

When she said, Ballard, I told her about my grassroots

activism. "I'm headed over to GOP headquarters now to meet up with some volunteers and make phone calls for the campaign," I said.

"Hang on," Heather said. "I want to give you something for Ballard."

She left the counter and walked out among the many shelves filled with hundreds of varieties of rocks in all colors, shapes and sizes. After a few minutes she returned.

"This stone is sodalite and works with the throat chakra. That will help Ballard to communicate clearly," she said, giving me a small blue and white stone.

I was loving the weirdness and felt excited, knowing I was smack inside another coincidence, a chance encounter that really wasn't chance at all.

"And this one is quartz." She plopped the second stone in my hand. "It will amplify his message and make sure it's received."

In the car I looked at the stones closely. I knew Ballard would appreciate the gesture and I couldn't wait to deliver them to him in person. I drove downtown to GOP headquarters and went inside. Before I knew it, I saw him walking toward me with a smile.

"Hello, Sir," I said. "I come bearing gifts." I showed him the stones and explained what each one meant. "They're charged and ready to go, Sir. Keep them in your pocket and you'll win."

The following week Ballard won in the biggest election upset in the history of Indiana politics. Some said it was the most surprising mayoral race upset in the country. A month after the election, Max and I drove to Chicago to accept an award from the Sam Adams Alliance for organizing a grassroots Tea Party movement in Indianapolis. It was one of the first Tea Party movements in the entire country. Then after a lengthy approval process, legislators opened the Indiana Constitution and placed a one percent cap on property tax.

As of 2013, the cap had saved taxpayers more than $1.5 billion.

TheDianaMythology

Months earlier, as part of the city's lawsuit, I had to host zoning inspectors again but this time at my house. The inspectors demanded access to my entire home and to be allowed to take pictures and measure every room. I had no legal choice but to consent to this invasion of privacy, so I decided to make a party of it. Because a new acquaintance from Detroit, Lornet Prather, was interested in the details of my lawsuit, I invited him to the day's festivities. He drove five hours, arriving before ten in the morning.

Lornet was a linguist and symbologist whom I met in late winter of 2006. He'd gone to my website and read a front page link entitled, "Miss Ann Defends the Indiana and US Constitutions." Lornet, whose nickname was Lonnie, left a cryptic message on my website guest book about Indiana being the home of the goddess Diana. "Thank you, Miss Ann, for defending freedom in Diana's Holy City," he wrote.

Rather than angrily greet my visitors from City Hall, I asked subJustin to serve them tea and cookies while wearing his collar. I also invited journalists from WIBC and *NUVO* to be on hand to document the city inspectors photographing every inch of my house. My lawyer, Mark, and a few other friends attended as well. All in all, I tried to make it fun rather than the grim reality it was–big brother's microscope in my personal space.

The zoning inspectors showed no emotion even though I had surprised them with a house full of people and two journalists. They said very little the whole time, just asked to go from room to room, measure and take pictures. That's all. When that was over, I asked Lonnie if he would enjoy a tour of Indianapolis to visit my sacred sites, as I called them.

Curious about the note he'd left regarding the goddess Diana, I found Lonnie had written extensively about the White Goddess which was something new and fascinating for me. His essays exalted early sexual revolutionaries like Mae West and Carole Lombard as well as other light-skinned blonds. I was hooked. The next thing I knew, we exchanged emails and were on the phone.

An interesting character to say the least, Lonnie was African-American and part of the Black Hebrew Israelite subculture of Judaism that believed they were direct descendants of the ancient Israelites. Lonnie had learned Hebrew and studied the Kabbalah which contained ancient Jewish teachings that defined reality, existence and the purpose of being. Numerology, derived from the Kabbalah, dealt with the significance of numbers and relationships between coincidental events.

A hospital psych nurse, Lonnie was at one time a male supremacist who prided himself on being a member of the superior sex. He felt it was his birthright to dominate, control and rule women and was an outspoken misogynist. A critic of Princess Diana of Wales, he had despised her cult-like following in the media and admirers around the globe. He fully dismissed as irrational the power she seemed to hold over the public.

Lonnie's spiritual conversion took place in a bookstore a few weeks after the death of Princess Diana. As he passed through the occult (Latin for hidden) section on his way to another area of the store, a sudden rush of energy knocked him to the ground. Lying motionless on the floor, he heard what he described absolutely as Princess Diana's voice in her soft British accent:

"Lonnie, Lonnie why did you persecute me?" she cried.

Those were the same words Paul heard on the road to Damascus at the time of his spiritual conversion. "Saul, Saul! Why do you persecute me?"

Hearing Princess Diana's voice, Lonnie instantly became aware that the history of women was mostly untold. His experience sounded a little implausible but I believed him. The message was so profound, it was impossible to dismiss its significance. History had recorded little of the past from a feminine point of view. Since the days the Goddess Diana was worshipped in Ephesus, histories of women, save a few like Catherine the Great and Queen Elizabeth I, had not been written down. Lonnie, an outspoken misogynist, had became aware in a single moment that there existed a missing side of history.

While most referred to her as Miss Victory, I called her Miss In-Diana as the newspapers had in the days following her official commemoration in 1902. Physically, she is the highest work of art in the state, a thirty-eight-foot liberty bronze that stands at the top of the Soldiers and Sailors Monument in Monument Circle. From the ground her details can hardly be seen. In her left hand Diana carries a torch of enlightenment. In her right, a sword of justice. She is the goddess of her city, In-Diana-polis, and I became immersed in her mythology.

My first encounter with Diana occurred during a 1989 visit to Ephesus, a city located nine miles from the bustling port of Kusadasi in Turkey on the Mediterranean Sea. In Greek mythology, the Goddess Diana of Ephesus was known as Artemis. An archer, she was goddess of the hunt and classically depicted protecting innocent deer. She swore never to marry, associated herself with chastity and functioned well independent of men.

Part of ancient Greece, Ephesus was the world's most cosmopolitan city in its day. It served as stomping grounds for Antony and Cleopatra and was home to the Virgin Mary.

During Jesus' lifetime, the Ephesians worshipped Diana. Several years after the crucifixion, Saul of Tarsus changed from a persecutor of Christ to Paul, the founder of Christianity. Paul's conversion could only be described as a supernatural experience. As he neared Damascus on his journey, suddenly a light from heaven flashed around him. He fell to the ground and heard a voice say to him,

> "Saul, Saul, why do you persecute me?"
> "Who are you, Lord?" Saul asked.
> "I am Jesus, whom you are persecuting," the voice replied. "Now get up and go into the city, and you will be told what you must do."
> The men traveling with Saul stood there speechless; they heard the sound but did not see anyone. Saul got up from the ground, but when he opened his eyes, he could see nothing. So they led him by the hand into Damascus. For three days he was blind and did not eat or drink anything. (Acts 9:3–9, *Holy Bible, New International Version*)

Paul then converted the Ephesians from Dianic worshipers to Christians–in other words, female deity worshippers converted to a patriarchal religion. Paul's beliefs were so radical that his views caused unrest and left him imprisoned in a tower near the sea. Afterward, worship of Diana was considered paganism. However, in ancient times paganism was all there was and predated Christianity.

I knew little about the city or ancient Greece at the time. I was taken to Ephesus on a Greek Island cruise and before departing Athens, my travel agent arranged for a counter-intelligence expert with the US Department of Defense to escort me to the port of Piraeus. Greece was tenuous at the time. In 1989, government employee strikes plagued the country and armed military personnel were positioned everywhere. My companion agreed to watch over me and became a dear friend and lover.

We disembarked from the ship and were directed to air-conditioned coaches that drove us to Ephesus. Minutes later, I found myself walking on a stone road with ancient grooves cut by chariot wheels, leading into the most magnificent place I'd ever seen.

Ephesus was home to one of the Seven Wonders of the Ancient World–the Temple of Artemis (Diana's Temple). One ionic column was all that remained to mark the site as ancient Ephesus had been destroyed by raids and buried by earthquakes. Archaeologists discovered the city in the late nineteenth century at the site of the vast amphitheater where Paul addressed the Ephesians. I felt a chemical surge the first time I entered the city though I had no idea why. My feelings seemed to come from a deeply emotional place that was my soul. I felt my spirit belonged in Ephesus and I never wanted to leave.

At one point, I almost dropped to my knees and my companion suggested we sit down. On the steps of the magnificent Celsus Library, I started crying. I could only explain that I was moved by the ruins. I wanted to be alone in the city, without all the tourists. For a short time, I was able to meditate inside the amphitheater but it wasn't enough. I needed clarity. Whatever was happening was profound and undefinable and I left mystified.

A few months after my trip, I swung by my downtown office in the King Cole Building a half block south of Monument Circle. On workdays I usually sat on the steps of the Soldiers and Sailors Monument and ate lunch. It was Saturday, and in those days back in the eighties, not many people were about. I strolled around the Circle and began to feel a kind of mystical beckoning. Then I heard as clear as a bell a voice in my mind.

"Do it! Do it now! Go ahead and just yell it!"

I looked around and saw a couple with their children crossing Market Street and a few people milling about.

"It's my city, I tell you! It's mine! It's mine!" the voice said.

I didn't know what to say or think. I tried to shrug it off as my wacky imagination.

"Do it! Say it!"

The voice was relentless, taunting me. The logic in my brain said if I shouted the words, I'd have a bed in the psych ward that night. Yet I couldn't resist. Unleashing the voice was the only way to free myself of it. I had to know what it felt like to act it out. I drew a deep breath.

"This is my city, I tell you! It's mine! It's mine!" I screamed as loudly as I could.

At that exact moment time seemed to freeze. The words roared from a place I'd never before felt inside myself. I looked around again but no one seemed to have noticed me shout. It was as if I existed in a supernatural bubble separate from the physical reality I occupied.

I didn't know what to make of what I had just done. On the surface, yelling at the top of my lungs in broad daylight was a preposterous thing to do. While the whisper of words in my head left me a bit unnerved, following its instructions freed me. Appeasing that voice began to unshackle me from my fears and insecurities. Maybe myths could not only be shared but they could also be experienced. Many years later, I began to believe I had encountered Diana's energy. The experience was profound though I might never fully understand it.

My first stop with Lornet was the Reflection Pond and Holcomb Gardens at Butler University. We climbed the sixty-two limestone steps to the Carillon Bell Tower, overlooking a reflection pond and spectacular fountain. The Tower is inscribed with a nineteenth century verse about music, a favorite by Henry Wadsworth Longfellow.

> And the night shall be filled with music,
> And the cares that infest the day,
> Shall fold their tents like the Arabs,
> And as silently steal away.
>
> —Henry Wadsworth Longfellow

We made our way down the steep hill to Holcomb Gardens and a nineteenth century French bronze of the Greek Goddess Persephone, Diana's half-sister. Zeus was their father. Standing alone in the center of a fountain, Persephone the goddess of vegetation, holds the same iconic torch carried by the Diana bronze atop Monument Circle downtown.

Next we drove to the nearby grounds of the Indianapolis Museum of Art. When I told Lonnie the property was once the home of the Lilly family of Lilly Pharmaceutical, he was awestruck. He recalled Princess Diana's coffin was covered with a spray of lilies, her most cherished flower. Hundreds of lilies, also my favorite, bloomed every summer in my own yard.

When I'd heard about Diana's death, I literally couldn't breathe for a moment and thought, "How can the world possibly go on without her in it?" Is that why admirers worldwide mourned for days? Such enormous grief could only be sparked by a powerful spirit. Had she been the flesh and blood incarnation of Diana? The White River flowed behind the Lilly Mansion, another connection with the White Goddess.

The tour seemed to be a long-awaited field trip for Lonnie. For years his studies were based in theory but that day he saw the symbology and interconnections he had envisioned. For Lonnie, everything fit. As we drove away from the IMA past the Christian Theological Seminary, I saw a deer in a grassy area near a small woods. Diana was classically depicted with deer. I slowed the car and as we drew closer, six or seven more deer emerged from the trees. It was unbelievable! In that moment I perceived the world of archetypes as real. We mortals have the ability to connect with it through the gift of our psyches. The chemical and emotional rush of this experience persisted all the way to our last stop.

We drove through Crown Hill Cemetery on a paved road winding among beautiful monuments and statuary. The famous and infamous are buried there: Eli Lilly, Robert Irsay, John Dillinger, President Benjamin Harrison and Indiana's famous children's poet, James Whitcomb Riley. My grandma had recited his famous poem, "Little Orphant Annie," to me each morning as she drove me to daycare. I always shrieked at the end.

> Little Orphant Annie's come to our house to stay,
> An' wash the cups an' saucers up, an' brush the crumbs away,
> An' shoo the chickens off the porch, an' dust the hearth,
> an' sweep,
> An' make the fire, an' bake the bread, an' earn her
> board-an'-keep;
> An' all us other childn, when the supper things is done,
> We set around the kitchen fire an' has the mostest fun
> A-list'nin' to the witch-tales 'at Annie tells about,
> An' the Gobble-uns 'at gits you
>
> Ef you
> Don't
> Watch
> Out!
>
> —James Whitcomb Riley

Riley's tomb was at the summit of the highest ground in Indianapolis. Driving up the hill was an adventure because the road seemed treacherously steep and curvy. Then the panoramic view from Riley's tomb at the city's peak felt like staring at heaven through a neo-classical Maxfield Parrish-esque lens.

"Only Diana's priestess could take me to heaven in her city," he said. "The spirit of Diana is everywhere."

As we drove back to my house, I tried to let everything sink in. Why had Lonnie really come? He'd never fully explained why he made the trip to Indianapolis. It seemed he had only come on a hunch.

"I've been looking for someone, Mely. When I fell down in the bookstore that day and heard the voice of Princess Diana," he said, "it seemed to have happened on purpose. Then I came across your site and saw what you were up against. I knew it was you."

"What are you talking about? What do you mean, me?" I asked.

"I've been looking for the dominatrix in your city. That's why I left you that message. In-Diana. In-Diana-polis. I've been looking for the powerful woman to fulfill the oracle set before me in the bookstore. What woman symbolizes more power than a dominatrix?"

I was listening.

"Everything I've researched has led me to you. This whole case is bigger than just you. It's about unearthing the spirit of Diana. You are it. You are the vehicle for her energy."

The day after Lonnie departed, I got on my computer to find out more about oracles. I learned they're portals through which the gods and goddesses speak to people.

I recalled the Hebrew word for God in Genesis, Elohim, a plural word that translates as "gods."

I finally saw the synchronicity, the coincidences connected by meaning in my life. Every strange twist and turn had led me to Diana. It sounded bizarre but the pieces fit snugly like a puzzle. My study of archetypes, the rush I experienced at each coincidence, the voices I heard, the tarot cards. It added up. I was the Queen of Wands. With trouble afoot, a queen sometimes finds there's no other choice but to go into battle herself. To achieve victory, I had to summon all my strength and energy to become a female knight, the rarest of all knights.

Epilogue

With a Lamp shall stand
In the great history of the land,
A noble type of good,
Heroic womanhood.

—Henry Wadsworth Longfellow

In April of 2011, Diana's bronze was lowered to undergo a $1.5 million restoration to mend her cracks and apply fresh gold leaf. The repairs were completed in a hangar at Indiana's military facility, Stout Field. In September, Diana returned to her home on Monument Circle. But coincidence struck once more. The plan to elevate the bronze was foiled as high winds kicked up, giving officials no choice but to leave her standing in a crate at street level for a week until the wind settled.

The whole thing was a spectacle. Citizens made pilgrimages to the capital all week to see her details up close. She was on the news every night. I visited Miss Victory each day to thank her archetype for giving me strength. She had provided me with courage to fight and win hard-fought battles with local government.

Without question, Diana rested on the Circle for a reason. To me, it was an opportunity for her spirit to intimately commune with the people. To most others, the reason was simply the weather.

Glossary
of People, Places and Terms

Abigail A generous artist neighbor who introduced me to the idea of a feng shui wealth area.

After The Ball–How America Will Conquer Its Fear and Hatred of Gays in the 90's by Marshall Kirk and Hunter Madsen. This book, written by two Harvard grads, a psychologist and an ad man, laid out a plan of unity and media strategy for the LGBT community.

Ajabu, Rev. Mmoja Ex-Black Panther and Minister of Social Concerns at an African-American church who commandeered a theatrical protest in a city council meeting.

Alan/Catbird The boyfriend who introduced me to D/s and with whom I started learning to be a domme. He is represented by the Knights of Wands tarot card.

Alex Founder of the Erotic Arts Show. A painter of nudes, he originally started the show to give kinky artists a place to display their work.

Alice A neighbor who helped me prepare the life-size salmon mousse lady for the 1997 Erotic Arts Show. I dubbed her butter bitch.

Allamel, Dr. Frédéric Judge for the Erotic Arts Ball exhibits. He wrote a book about the erotic art and artifact collection of Dr. Alfred Kinsey in the Kinsey Institute at Indiana University.

Antonio A dom friend who lived in my house during my transition to professional dominatrix. He was a steadfast friend and stabilizing influence during rough times.

Arie A D/s lifestyle pal from Cincinnati who helped me unwind after being outed.

Aaron A great friend who established my legal defense fund and matched every donation dollar for dollar out of his own pocket.

Ballard, Greg Mayoral candidate who upset Bart Peterson in the election of 2007.

Barry, Uncle A longtime non-kinky friend. He asked me to make the salmon mousse lady for the 1997 Erotic Arts show, leased me space in the Chatham Center and gave me support during my lawsuit.

Bateman, Paul A city councilman.

BDSM Bondage-Discipline-Sadism-Masochism.

Bond, Dave Founder of S.T.O.P. Indiana and a political activist in my circle.

Brenner, Greg Showed up for me at the mayor's press conference on the subject of my lawsuit from the city. Band promoter and host of Indy's legendary punk band night held on Saturdays at the historic Melody Inn.

Butler-Tarkington A neighborhood named after Butler University and Indiana writer Booth Tarkington.

Byron The pilot who flew to Indy from California to lifestyle scene with me. Our interaction was so intense, we ended up spending five days together. Byron gave me permission as a domme to be as brutal with him as I wished.

CB2000 A plastic male chastity device that prevents erection.

Celestine Prophecy, The This best-selling book by James Redfield made me aware of synchronicity and the significance of life's coincidences.

Central Canal Eight miles of historic canal and towpath running through the heart of Indianapolis from the White River in Broad Ripple Village to downtown Indianapolis. The path is home to wildlife, especially ducks, geese, blue cranes and a ton of large water turtles. It's used daily for recreational purposes by walkers, joggers and bicyclists. It was the site of Indiana's first tea party.

Chatham Center Located in an historic downtown neighborhood called Chatham Arch near Massachusetts Avenue. I rented space there from Uncle Barry for my kinky boutique.

Chatterbox My all-time favorite dive bar located on Mass Ave. The Chatterbox has hosted some of the most famous jazz artists in America.

Christina/Mistress Claudia A young woman who rented a room in my house. Turned out she was a hardcore sadist, wanted to be a professional domme and asked me to be her madame.

Cindy My younger sister. We had different fathers and grew up with our unmarried mom in Palmerton, Indiana.

COIT County Option Income Tax. In 2007, Mayor Peterson announced an increase in the COIT about the same time homeowners were getting outrageous property reassessments from the state. We used the COIT hike to target the mayor in our protests over the exorbitant state property tax increases. People went ballistic and lines were blurred. Some taxpayers blamed the city's mayor for the state property tax fiasco.

Daniels, Mitch Indiana governor from 2005-2012, in office during the property tax crisis. He said the state had mishandled property reassessments and put a halt to all tax payments until the problem was resolved.

Depeche Mode A 1980s English band that recorded "Master and Servant."

Derek A crazy, brilliant boyfriend I met at a fetish party. Derek was elegant, original and daring, all characteristics that made him a magnet for me. I loved it that he was wild and outrageous. I wanted to be able to count on him but the relationship couldn't survive the differences between us.

Don An undercover cop sent by the city to try to entrap me for prostitution. I played out a D/s scene with him and refused to give him what he wanted.

Droid An online sub I counseled regarding his real life D/s relationship. He flew me to Seattle for a vacation to meet him.

D/s Dominance and submission.

Erotic Arts Ball Name of the Erotic Arts Show for the tenth anniversary in 2004. I was proud of the huge success of this ball and learned organizational skills from the year it took me to put it together.

Fetish An unusual sexual desire linked to an object, clothing or part of the body. Examples are a foot fetish, bondage, spanking and sex toys.

Flipper An outspoken retired firefighter who was an activist and personal driver for mayoral candidate Greg Ballard.

Fluttering Menace An experienced domme who was both a friend and antagonist. I admired her in the beginning but later she turned on me for reasons I never fully understood.

Footbytch A sub I offered a lifestyle position in service to my foot care.

Gil/Latex Kitten Gil made the steel cross that I bought for my dungeon. He came to live in my house for a while and served as my latex pet.

Grandma The most influential person in my life who taught me values and honor. I feel that her light lives on in me every day.

Gray, Monroe City council president.

Governor's Mansion The location of my first tax rally on Meridian Street located in the center of my neighborhood.

Greta A man who lived secretly as a cross-dresser and wrote about his life in my Yahoo! forum.

Gustafson, Chris A fetish photographer from Detroit who came to Indy to do a photo shoot in my dungeon with Sydney and Master Scott. We later did a shoot on the Monon Trail of me walking my latex pet.

High Jinx An Indy strip club with a fetish night where I found Sydney/Liza.

Horning, Andy A constitutionalist and guru within the Libertarian Party who often spoke at protests and demonstrations. Andy was my go-to policy guy.

Howey, Brian Founded the Howey Political Report, a publication that followed my story.

IMA I walked often in the Indianapolis Museum of Art gardens for inspiration and serenity. I believe it is Diana's garden.

IndyErnie An activist at the Tea Party rally at the Central Canal who founded the effective "Bart Lies" campaign.

InKink A local kink organization that I wanted to help grow. I hoped to bring kinky people together the same way gays had united and legitimized their community.

INtake An *Indianapolis Star* subsidiary that published a glowing report about the Erotic Arts Ball.

Ishmael The electrician who did the lighting in my dungeon and wanted to be paid by being spanked with a hair brush.

Janet A college student in the kink goth crowd who organized a monthly fetish party at a downtown nightclub.

Jeff The commodities trader I drove to Chicago to lifestyle scene with. He took me to check out a public dungeon. Watching people there made me realize I never wanted to scene in public.

Jeopardy bondage Being tied up with knots rigged to tighten when the submissive struggles.

Jonathan The Army Ranger novice sub who drove out from Virginia to scene with me.

Julie A well-liked domme who helped me kill my Miss Ann persona.

Justin A young bondage submissive who entered my service at my boutique. He was a sweet boy I grew fond of.

Katrianna A total power exchange (TPE) domme who reigned over the old guard Master/slave scene.

Kaye, Jennifer A local art curator who helped me hang exhibits at the Erotic Arts Ball.

Keith Gay and a blast to be around, Keith had a downtown persona and was the perfect city roommate for me in the nineties. His friends were campy and brainy and I loved going with him on his party circuit.

Kendrick, Teri City Prosecutor when the city sued me.

King, Kim A local news reporter from Fox 59 who came to my home to interview me.

Lady Liza/Sydney The subject of a bondage photo shoot and a dominatrix trainee in my dungeon.

Legal Beagle A downtown gathering place for Fair Tax plan enthusiasts frequented by lawyers,

Liam/TiedUpToday A submissive who introduced me to bondage and encouraged me to be a professional dominatrix.

Lilly Mansion Former home of the Lilly family, a mansion on the grounds of the Indianapolis Museum of Art.

Living Room Lounge The bar off Pennsylvania Avenue where the Tea Party was hatched.

Lunar Event A popular local band that played at my boutique's grand opening.

Mass Ave The cultural district downtown where I networked with the arts crowd.

Master Scott Sydney's slave master.

Max My young activist boyfriend went to all my meetings with me and moved in to provide protection because he felt that as an activist leader I was exposed.

Melody Inn One of my favorite Indy bars that hosts Punk Rock Night every Saturday. They partenered with the Erotic Arts Ball.

Meridian-Kessler The 1920's north Indianapolis neighborhood where I lived.

MistressHouston My online nemesis who outed me to the police and media in Indianapolis.

MistressMadeline An online domme I made fun of by calling her MotelMaddy.

MistressSatin An online domme I satirized, renaming her MistressFatten.

Mitch My detective neighbor knew about my kinky life and helped out when I built my dungeon.

Monon Trail An asphalted rail trail through Indianapolis for walkers, runners and cyclists. This was the place chosen for a photo shoot of me with latex kitten on a leash.

Murat Theatre Originally a Shrine temple that became an entertainment venue, the oldest stage house in downtown Indy.

NCSF National Coalition for Sexual Freedom.

Neal An understanding friend who listened when my relationship with Derek was disintegrating.

Nicky Blaine's A martini bar where Abdul hosted a happy hour for his followers.

Niles A loyal friend and one of the few subs I worked with who was into the pure psychological aspects of D/s.

NUVO An alternative Indy newspaper for whom Paul Pogue reported.

O'Neal, Sean A director of the Fair Tax movement in Indiana who helped with unfair tax rallies.

Orentlicher, David An IU law professor and three-term democratic state legislator.

OWK Other World Kingdom, a commercial BDSM and femdom facility located in the Czech Republic, opened in 1997.

Patriot Paul Became a memorable symbol for the cause in his authentic colonial costume. He became a sort of local celebrity because of the many times he was filmed and photographed.

Peterson, Bart The popular mayor of Indianapolis whom I helped to defeat in the 2007 election.

Pigtails Served as a sissy maid in my house for over a year. He was a burly truck driver who craved feminization and got his name when I put his long hair in pigtails.

Pogue, Paul An award-winning journalist with NUVO who wrote a true account of what happened when I was outed and the media and police showed up at my house.

Prather, Lornet A linguist and symbologist from Detroit who was important to me in finding out more about the Goddess Diana.

Princess William A wealthy sub from Chicago who asked me to play out his extreme blackmail fantasy.

Quintana, Pastor Joe A former NYC cop who presided over an inner city church and was an activist in the tax protests.

Rachael Owned a local custom corset-business, Surrean Designs. Rachael put on a theatrical performance with models acting out naughty nursery rhymes in her corsetry at the Erotic Arts Ball.

Radford One of my best non-kinky friends who brought a busload of costumed friends to see my dungeon on Halloween and served as emcee of The Erotic Arts Ball. Radford referred to me to my lawyer, Mark Small.

Red Key Tavern A 1930's original bar near my Meridian-Kessler house. No ferns in this bar. It was the site of my first date with Catbird.

Reformatory, The My D/s boutique in Chatham Arch, a downtown cultural district near Mass Ave.

Rehagen, Tony Shadowed me for about a month before the 2007 election. He wrote a story for *The Indianapolis Monthly* about my metamorphosis from dominatrix to political activist.

Rinehart, Jack A crime beat reporter from WRTV 6. He followed up on a tip sent to him in an outrageous and untrue press release and showed up with a cameraman at my house, asking for an interview.

Rowe, Mike A local realtor and activist who initiated the Black Sunday rally.

Rutherford, Mark Former chair of Indiana's Libertarian Party.

Shibari An intricate method of knot tying that in D/s circles means Japanese rope bondage.

Soldiers and Sailors Monument A neoclassical war monument in the center of Indianapolis.

Sanders, JoAnne A city councilwoman.

Scotsman The creative activist who planned the Breakfast at Bart's protest and had the best ideas for signs and scenarios, working always on the front lines.

Shabazz, Abdul-Hakim A radio host and African-American with Muslim heritage who helped me get out my side of the story after the lawsuit.

Shepard, Sean A director of Fair Tax in Indiana with whom I worked as an activist. He helped lead rallies.

SirSissy An online sub who played the role of chat room antagonist in Dominant Women and became my partner in crime when I created The Herd website.

Small, Mark My lawyer during the lawsuit who loved a good constitutional rights fight.

Spangle, Chris Former Executive Director of the Indiana Libertarian Party, who coined activists as the Justice League.

Sparrow She helped me write my press release after the Channel 6 news report to try to get the straight story out to the public. Building InKink to qualify for affiliation with NCSF was her pet project.

Stevie DJ from the goth scene who took over the fetish parties that evolved into charity events.

Synchronicity Coincidences that have no discernible causal relationship but are connected by meaning.

Talbott Street A downtown gay bar and nightclub with dancing and drag shows. They gave us space for the Fair Tax 101 forum.

Ted An offbeat musical genius who created the soundtrack for the Erotic Art Ball's reception.

Thacher My struggling ceramic artist boyfriend in the late nineties. He had a goofy sense of humor and loved the children he taught to work with clay. I bought an old Craftsman-style house and we moved in together.

Three Graces A lovely marble sculpture at the IMA that depicts a D/s scene.

TPE Total power exchange. In TPE the sub gives all his power to a domme who makes every life decision for him.

Trigger the Human Equine The man with the soul of a horse who gave rides on his shoulder saddle at the Erotic Arts Ball.

Utne Reader An alternative news magazine where I first saw Marianne Williamson's poem.

Welsh, Gary A former lobbyist and local attorney who wrote the blog Advance Indiana.

Trevor A sub who worked as a slave, building the dungeon. He craved humiliation.

Ziegler, Connie A local historian and Mass Ave business owner who put on an historical undergarments fashion show at the Erotic Arts Ball, with models wearing girdles and bullet brassieres.